UNLOCKING THE POTENTIAL OF RAILWAYS
A Railway Strategy for CAREC, 2017–2030

Endorsed at the 15th CAREC Ministerial Conference
Islamabad, Pakistan, 26 October 2016

 Creative Commons Attribution 3.0 IGO license (CC BY 3.0 IGO)

© 2017 Asian Development Bank
6 ADB Avenue, Mandaluyong City, 1550 Metro Manila, Philippines
Tel +63 2 632 4444; Fax +63 2 636 2444
www.adb.org

Some rights reserved. Published in 2017.
Printed in the Philippines.

ISBN 978-92-9257-747-6 (Print), 978-92-9257-748-3 (e-ISBN)
Publication Stock No. RPT178656-2
DOI: http://dx.doi.org/10.22617/RPT178656-2

Cataloging-In-Publication Data

Asian Development Bank.
    Unlocking the potential of railways: A railway strategy for CAREC, 2017–2030.
Mandaluyong City, Philippines: Asian Development Bank, 2017.

1. CAREC.   2. Railway.   3. Strategy.   I. Asian Development Bank.

The views expressed in this publication are those of the authors and do not necessarily reflect the views and policies of the Asian Development Bank (ADB) or its Board of Governors or the governments they represent.

ADB does not guarantee the accuracy of the data included in this publication and accepts no responsibility for any consequence of their use. The mention of specific companies or products of manufacturers does not imply that they are endorsed or recommended by ADB in preference to others of a similar nature that are not mentioned.

By making any designation of or reference to a particular territory or geographic area, or by using the term "country" in this document, ADB does not intend to make any judgments as to the legal or other status of any territory or area.

This work is available under the Creative Commons Attribution 3.0 IGO license (CC BY 3.0 IGO) https://creativecommons.org/licenses/by/3.0/igo/. By using the content of this publication, you agree to be bound by the terms of this license.

This CC license does not apply to non-ADB copyright materials in this publication. If the material is attributed to another source, please contact the copyright owner or publisher of that source for permission to reproduce it. ADB cannot be held liable for any claims that arise as a result of your use of the material.

Attribution—You should always acknowledge ADB as the source using the following format:
    [Author]. [Year of publication]. [Title of the work in italics]. [City of publication]: [Publisher]. © ADB. [URL or DOI] [license].

Translations—Any translations you create should carry the following disclaimer:
    Originally published by ADB in English under the title [title in italics]. © ADB. [URL or DOI] [license]. The quality of the translation and its coherence with the original text is the sole responsibility of the translator. The English original of this work is the only official version.

Adaptations—Any adaptations you create should carry the following disclaimer:
    This is an adaptation of an original work titled [title in italics]. © ADB. [URL or DOI][license]. The views expressed here are those of the authors and do not necessarily reflect the views and policies of ADB or its Board of Governors or the governments they represent. ADB does not endorse this work or guarantee the accuracy of the data included in this publication and accepts no responsibility for any consequence of their use.

Please contact pubsmarketing@adb.org if you have questions or comments with respect to content, or if you wish to obtain copyright permission for your intended use that does not fall within these terms, or for permission to use the ADB logo.

Notes:
In this publication, "$" refers to US dollars.
ADB recognizes "China" as the People's Republic of China.
Corrigenda to ADB publications may be found at http://www.adb.org/publications/corrigenda

 Printed on recycled paper

Contents

Tables, Figures, Boxes, and Maps	iv
Foreword	v
Preface	vi
Abbreviations	vii
Executive Summary	viii
CHAPTER 1: Background and Rationale	**1**
Trade Flows	1
Future of Subregional Trade	3
Comparative Advantages of Rail over Other Modes of Transport	3
CHAPTER 2: CAREC Railway Assessment	**5**
Considerable Infrastructure Needs	5
Constraints on Public Finance for Railways	5
Key Railway Reform Experience	6
CHAPTER 3: A Railway Strategy for CAREC	**9**
Vision: CAREC Railways to Become the Transport Mode of Choice by 2030	9
Priorities	10
CHAPTER 4: Preliminary Action Plan	**11**
Effective Infrastructure Investments	11
Robust Commercial Capacity	14
Institutional, Legal, and Regulatory Initiatives	19
CHAPTER 5: Implementing the Strategy	**22**
Mobilize and Leverage Sufficient Financing	22
Building Capacity	23
Transfer of Technology	23
Appendixes	**24**
1 Results-Based Framework	24
2 Central Asia Regional Economic Cooperation Railway Map	26
3 Designated Rail Corridors	28
4 Priority Investment Projects	42
5 Rail Infrastructure Project Prioritization Methodology	46
6 CAREC Railway Data	53

Tables, Figures, Boxes, and Maps

Tables

A3.1	CAREC Designated Rail Corridors: Summary of Technical Features	41
A4.1	List of Railway Investment Projects	43
A5.1	Example Matrix of Nonmonetizable and/or Nonquantified Effects	48
A5.2	Example Effects Matrix and Project Ranking	49
A5.3	Average External Costs in 2008 for EU-27 by Cost Category and Transport Mode (Excluding Congestion)	52
A6.1	CAREC Railway Data, 2014	53

Figures

1	CAREC 9 Exports to Trade Partners, 2015	2
2	CAREC 9 Imports from Trade Partners, 2015	2
3	Global Competitiveness Index and Rail Infrastructure Quality Rankings for Selected CAREC Countries	4
4	Vision, Approach, and Priorities	9
5	Specialized CAREC Carriers	17
6	CAREC Corridor Management and Service Design	18
A4.1	Distribution of Investments by Implementation Period	42
A4.2	Distribution of Investments by Country, 2017–2020	42
A4.3	Distribution of Investments by Corridor, 2017–2020	42
A5.1	Three Spheres of Sustainability	47
A5.2	People–Planet–Profit Diagram Applied to an Infrastructure Project	47

Boxes

1	Railway Reform in Kazakhstan	7
2	Alternative Financing Mechanisms for Railway Development in the People's Republic of China	22

Maps

1	Central Asia Regional Economic Cooperation Designated Rail Corridors	13
A3.1	Central Asia Regional Economic Cooperation Designated Rail Corridor 1: Europe–East Asia	29
A3.2	Central Asia Regional Economic Cooperation Designated Rail Corridor 2: Mediterranean–East Asia	31
A3.3	Central Asia Regional Economic Cooperation Designated Rail Corridor 3: Russian Federation–Middle East and South Asia	34
A3.4	Central Asia Regional Economic Cooperation Designated Rail Corridor 4: Russian Federation–East Asia	35
A3.5	Central Asia Regional Economic Cooperation Designated Rail Corridor 5: East Asia–Middle East and South Asia	37
A3.6	Central Asia Regional Economic Cooperation Designated Rail Corridor 6: Europe–Middle East and South Asia	39

Foreword

International trade enriches its participants. Ever since Adam Smith and David Ricardo, economists have associated increases in international trade with economic growth, higher incomes, and improvements in human conditions. International trade depends on robust transport systems. Inadequate transport infrastructure, poor network integration, difficult border procedures, and poor or irregular service levels hinder trade and economic growth.

The level of economic and transport development differs greatly among Central Asian Regional Economic Cooperation (CAREC) countries. CAREC countries face different challenges in upgrading and enhancing transport networks and improving their integration. In particular, the extent to which rail transport is used and the maturity of intermodal linkages varies widely. Differential economic growth, changing trade patterns, and local developments in transport structures change the demands on and for rail freight transport. Rapid increases in trade, and changes in the geographic and commodity structure of trade flows require actions to adapt the railway industry (infrastructure, facilities, and services) to suit new requirements. CAREC countries are also at different stages in devising strategies to remedy rail sector deficiencies and planning for future needs.

Regional cooperation in railway development can contribute to increased interregional and intraregional trade in the subregion. There is common recognition by member countries, industry, and the general public of the benefits that an integrated CAREC railway system can deliver: expanding trade and improving economic development of CAREC economies. This is exactly the goal specified in the CAREC Transport and Trade Facilitation Strategy 2020, which aims to develop the region's multimodal transport network, improve trade and border crossing services, and improve operational and institutional effectiveness.

The drive toward an efficient and more competitive CAREC railway network received strong support at the 15th CAREC Ministerial Conference in Islamabad in October 2016. CAREC can have an important role in the development of an integrated transport and trade facilitation framework, serving the CAREC vision of *Good Neighbors, Good Partners, and Good Prospects*.

Unlocking the Potential of Railways: A Railway Strategy for CAREC, 2017–2030 is intended to inform policy makers of the importance of the development of railways, and contribute to the ongoing dialogue on regional economic cooperation in the CAREC region. The Asian Development Bank, as the secretariat of the CAREC program, looks forward to deepening its engagement with CAREC member countries in their implementation of this Strategy.

Takehiko Nakao
President
Asian Development Bank

Preface

The Transport and Trade Facilitation Strategy 2020 (TTFS 2020), endorsed by Central Asia Regional Economic Cooperation (CAREC) member countries in 2013, focuses on the development of an effective, efficient, sustainable, safe, and user-friendly multimodal corridor network to expand trade and accelerate economic growth. The TTFS 2020 recognized the importance of railways in completing this multimodal corridor network.

The TTFS 2020 recognized that fully developing the CAREC railway network will continue well beyond the 2020 planning horizon, given the large investments required. Many proposed railway projects are not yet capable of attracting financing from purely commercial sources. They require financial assistance from governments and international financial institutions, which need to ensure that the investments are financially viable and help railway organizations to carry out reforms to make them more efficient and financially sustainable.

In light of the above, *Unlocking the Potential of Railways: A Railway Strategy for CAREC, 2017–2030* has been formulated by CAREC member countries to serve as a guiding document for the sound, long-term development of CAREC railways. The Strategy is intended to equip the region's railways to better capture evolving trade flows and contribute to regional economic development.

The Strategy was formulated by the Railway Working Group (RWG), which was set up by the decision of the 14th Transport Sector Coordinating Committee in Ulaanbaatar in April 2015. The RWG consists of representatives of railway agencies from CAREC member countries, supported by expert organizations such as the Organization for Cooperation of Railways and International Union Railways, as well as CAREC development partners. The RWG convened in Tokyo in November 2015, and in Bangkok in April 2016 where countries shared their status, plans, and issues regarding railways and agreed on the vision, priorities, and actions underpinning the Strategy.

The Asian Development Bank's secretariat team for the development of the Strategy was led by Xiaohong Yang, Director, Transport and Communications Division of the Central and West Asia Department. The team consisted of Takeshi Fukayama, Jurgen Sluijter, Ko Sakamoto, Oleg Samukhin, Joseph Procak, Ghia Villareal, Ma. Corazon Cecilia Sison, Maria Cecilia Villanueva, and Alice Arenas-Poblete; and was supported by John Winner, Richard Bullock, Thomas Kennedy, Paul Power, Nelson Alvarez, Pilarcita Sahilan, and Debbie Gundaya (consultants). Further guidance was provided by Tyrrell Duncan, Technical Advisor (Transport), Sector Advisory Service Cluster of the Sustainable Development and Climate Change Department, and Robert Guild, Director, Transport and Communications Division of the East Asia Department. The team was supported by staff and consultants from numerous other divisions and resident missions.

It is our sincere hope that the Strategy will be implemented by the countries for the sound development of the railways in the region.

Sean O'Sullivan
Director General
Central and West Asia Department
Asian Development Bank

Ayumi Konishi
Director General
East Asia Department
Asian Development Bank

Abbreviations

ADB	–	Asian Development Bank
ADB–ARIC	–	Asian Development Bank–Asian Regional Integration Center
BCP	–	border crossing point
CAREC	–	Central Asia Regional Economic Cooperation
CBA	–	cost–benefit analysis
CER	–	Community of European Railway and Infrastructure Companies
CIS	–	Commonwealth of Independent States
CPMM	–	Corridor Performance Measurement and Monitoring
DRC	–	designated rail corridor
EAEU	–	Eurasian Economic Union
ECO	–	Economic Cooperation Organization
EU	–	European Union
GDP	–	gross domestic product
IFI	–	international financial institution
IFRS	–	international financial reporting standards
JSC KTZ	–	Joint Stock Company Kazakhstan Temir Zholy (Joint Stock Company Kazakhstan National Railway)
JSC RZD	–	Rossiiskie Zheleznye Dorogi (Joint Stock Company Russian Railways)
MCA	–	multi-criteria analysis
OSJD	–	Organization for Cooperation of Railways
RWG	–	railway working group
TTFS	–	Transport and Trade Facilitation Strategy
UIC	–	Union Internationale des Chemins de Fer (International Union of Railways)
UTLC	–	United Transport Logistics Company

Executive Summary

Currently about 25,000 kilometers of main railway corridors in and outside the CAREC region connect the countries within the region. However, the existing rail network does not necessarily match the changing trade patterns it is meant to serve. Growing export and import activity with the People's Republic of China and Europe are not currently being served. Railways have the potential to transform the region from being landlocked into being land-linked and connecting it better with its rapidly growing neighbors. Although rail infrastructure has contributed in maintaining the competitiveness of the countries that are in CAREC, its quality needs to be improved so that the improved railways will facilitate increased regional cooperation and integration.

The vision behind the CAREC railway strategy is to see to it that rail transport will become the preferred mode of choice for trade: quick, efficient, accessible to customers, and easy to use throughout the region. To achieve this vision, a number of priorities have been formulated for the following three primary efforts: (i) to develop effective rail infrastructure; (ii) to develop robust commercial capabilities; and (iii) to improve legal and regulatory frameworks.

Priority rail infrastructure investments will be needed to (i) fill gaps and missing links in existing networks, (ii) renovate important segments of existing rail infrastructure, (iii) modernize and replace rolling stock, and (iv) modernize information technologies. To help prioritize the infrastructure investments, the Strategy identifies Designated Railway Corridors and a methodology for prioritizing specific investment projects.

Most shippers find it difficult to conduct commercial transactions with railways—it is more difficult to deal with multiple railways for international shipments. The development of a range of commercial responses can make rail transport more comprehensible, easier to arrange, and more attractive. To this end, the Strategy includes such actions as (i) single point of contact, (ii) formation of CAREC rail operators, (iii) bulk/logistics terminal improvements, (iv) joint locomotive leasing, and (v) formation of corridor management units with the capability of integrating service design across corridor railways.

As a part of the continuing evolution of the economic development of CAREC countries, some governments may wish to transition the legal framework of their national railways from one form to another. Actions identified to effect such changes include (i) institutional transition, (ii) tariff deregulation, (iii) International Financial Reporting Standards and cost accounting modifications, and (iv) customs and border control improvement.

The Strategy recognizes that the full implementation of the aforementioned actions requires a set of robust arrangements addressing funding (financing), people (capacity), and technology.

CHAPTER 1
Background and Rationale

1. Economic and political developments in the Central Asia Regional Economic Cooperation (CAREC) region over the last two decades have radically changed the structure of the economies and patterns of trade flows. The region's institutions and economies continue to evolve, and trade flows continue to change in response. Since rail networks have long lives, existing network configurations do not necessarily match new traffic patterns; many railways in the region are struggling to adapt to these changing conditions. Railway market shares have generally declined and most railways are not fully participating in available trade flows. In particular, much freight traffic is carried by roads rather than rail (especially intermediate products and finished goods for longer distance), costing the economy more than it should. As a result, interregional and intraregional trade faces high transportation costs and bottlenecks. A regional railway system improved by infrastructure investments and reforms will help shift freight traffic back to rail, reducing transport costs and helping to increase economic growth and social welfare.

2. Railways must adapt their regional networks and institutional structures to changing transport patterns. However, many railway investment projects are currently not bankable using normal commercial mechanisms.[1] They do not satisfy criteria used by commercial banks for financial sustainability. Hence, there is a need to seek alternative financing and funding mechanisms, including external assistance from both government and international financial institutions (IFIs). The institutional and commercial changes needed to improve financial sustainability are difficult to implement. The focus of the CAREC strategy is to equip the region's railways to address these issues so they can better capture evolving trade flows and contribute to regional economic development.

3. Increasing concerns about energy security, the adverse effects of road transport on road spending needs, and the environmental impacts of road transport have also made the region more appreciative of the role of railways as an inexpensive, efficient, safe, and environmentally sound mode of transport.

Trade Flows

4. Most of the CAREC countries are landlocked.[2] The CAREC program aims to help transform CAREC countries from landlocked to land-linked status, expanding trade and improving economic development by more closely connecting the CAREC Region with its larger and rapidly growing neighbors. Central Asia has great potential to benefit from growing Eurasian and global transit traffic and the intraregional trade which will develop in the coming decades. Improving the ability of railways to move freight traffic at low cost and with a small environmental footprint will contribute to the expansion of trade in landlocked countries.

5. The CAREC 9 countries[3] export mostly to the European Union (EU) (33% of all exports in 2015) and the People's Republic of China (PRC) (19%). CAREC 9 countries exports are growing more rapidly into the PRC (22% per year from 2000 to

---

[1] Many rail projects are less bankable because (i) long gestation periods, (ii) tariffs too low to recover the large amount of investment, and (iii) high external effects such as environmental and social benefits, which are difficult to internalize. Because of these characteristics, many railway projects are economically viable but not financially or commercially viable.

[2] CAREC countries include Afghanistan, Azerbaijan, the People's Republic of China (PRC), Georgia, Kazakhstan, the Kyrgyz Republic, Mongolia, Pakistan, Tajikistan, Turkmenistan, and Uzbekistan.

[3] The term CAREC 9 refers to the CAREC member countries except for PRC and Georgia. EU includes Austria, Belgium, Bulgaria, Cyprus, Czech Republic, Denmark, Estonia, Finland, France, Germany, Greece, Hungary, Ireland, Italy, Latvia, Lithuania, Luxembourg, Malta,

2015). The next fastest growing exports are within the CAREC 9 community (15% per year). Exports to the EU, Middle East and South Asia all grew at 11% per year. These are shown in Figure 1.

6. As indicated in Figure 2, most imports coming into the CAREC 9 countries come from the PRC (25% of all imports in 2015); it is also the fastest growing source of imports (more than 30% per

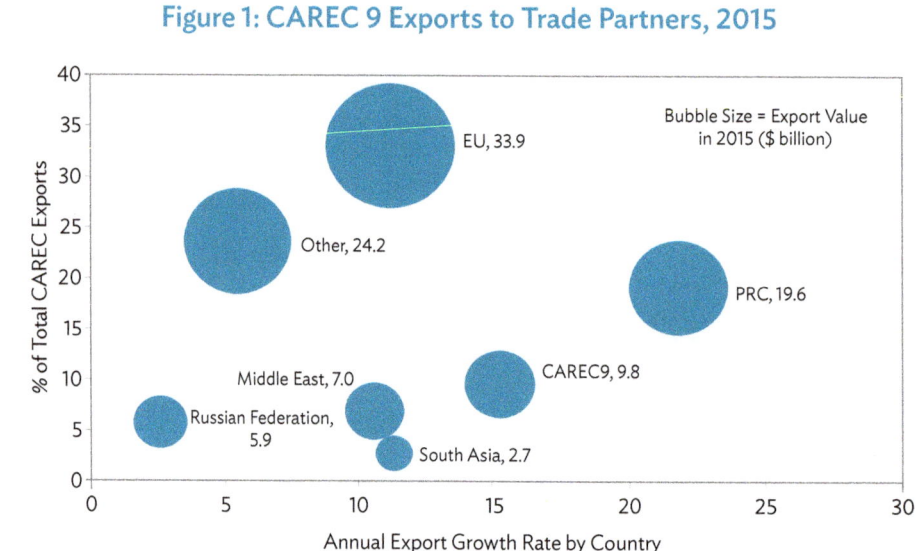

Figure 1: CAREC 9 Exports to Trade Partners, 2015

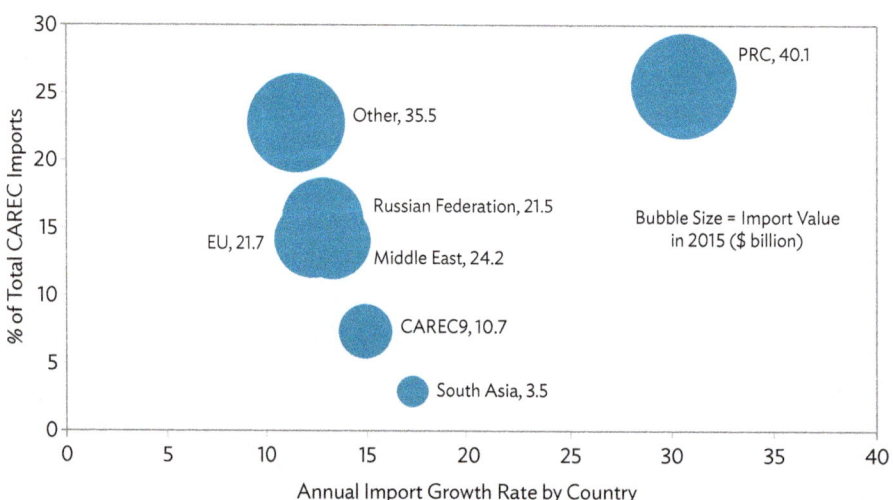

Figure 2: CAREC 9 Imports from Trade Partners, 2015

CAREC = Central Asia Regional Economic Cooperation, PRC = People's Republic of China, EU = European Union.
Note: Annual growth rate is that between 2000 and 2015, based on the nominal dollar value of CAREC9 imports and exports (excluding the PRC).
Source: ADB Calculations using data from ADB-ARIC, International Monetary Fund. *Direction of Trade and Statistics.* https://aric.adb.org/integrationindicators (accessed 9 September 2016).

the Netherlands, Poland, Portugal, Romania, Slovak Republic, Slovenia, Spain, Sweden, and the United Kingdom. Middle East consists of Kingdom of Bahrain, Egypt, Islamic Republic of Iran, Iraq, Jordan, Kuwait, Lebanon, Libya, Mauritania, Oman, Qatar, Saudi Arabia, Syrian Arab Republic, United Arab Emirates, and Republic of Yemen. South Asia refers to Bangladesh, Bhutan, India, the Maldives, Nepal, and Sri Lanka. Others refer to the rest of the world.

year). Imports from the EU, the Middle East, and the Russian Federation all grew at about 13% per year. The import shares of these trading partners in 2015 were also roughly comparable—13% to 15%. The PRC is CAREC 9's fastest growing export and import market.[4]

7. International trade flows have slowed in recent years as demand for a wide range of raw materials typically carried by railways has declined. The impact of these changes is reflected in the significant decline in prices for oil and many other basic commodities. Future growth projections for large parts of the world economy have been scaled back in recent months. The current global economic landscape, with lower primary commodity prices, lower remittances, and slower economic growth is creating immediate additional difficulties for a number of CAREC countries. Slower economic growth and low prices for raw materials and basic industrial products are expected to continue to affect rail freight traffic for several more years.

Future of Subregional Trade

8. Central Asia lies at the heart of the ancient Silk Route. Sparsely populated and with vast resources, trade is vital to CAREC countries. Both intra-regional and extra-regional trade has great potential to grow if bottlenecks, logistics and supply-chain challenges can be addressed. Since the time of the ancient Silk Road, intra- and interregional trade have made a significant contribution to the economies of the region. However, long distance travel, high mountains and deserts constitute formidable barriers to transport and trade in the region. Most international trade relies on land transport through the territories of multiple neighboring countries requiring cooperation and closer integration of rail transport systems. In countries like Kazakhstan and the PRC, which have worked on increasing cooperation and closer integration for many years, containers in block trains are becoming increasingly cost competitive with sea and air transport for high-value trade flows.

9. In the current difficult global economic environment, CAREC countries will need to further strengthen regional cooperation and integration efforts. Investment in railway assets (including freight cars and locomotives) and implementation of related soft measures to enhance trade will be critical factors in making railways attractive for shippers and transport operators. Enhancing railway connectivity, promoting trade and investment across borders, and improving access to external markets will help improve the economic prospects of the subregion as a whole. As the structure of the economies in the region shift toward more services, railways should focus on high-value services. Since trade between CAREC countries is among the fastest growing, railways should work to attract shorter-haul international traffic between CAREC countries.

Comparative Advantages of Rail Over Other Modes of Transport

10. Regional cooperation in rail transport can help participating countries diversify trade patterns. Improvements in rail transport can also help attract foreign direct investment, increase participation in global production networks, increase related trade in manufactured products, and diversify exports.

11. The World Economic Forum's Global Competitiveness Report evaluates the competitiveness of countries based on the Global Competitiveness Index. One of the pillars of the competitiveness index is infrastructure. As indicated in Figure 3, among the eight CAREC countries (including Georgia) that the report analyzes, the quality of rail infrastructure is weak except for those in the PRC and Kazakhstan, both of which have

---

[4] Source for data in charts: ADB Calculations using data from ADB-ARIC, Direction of Trade and Statistics, International Monetary Fund. Annual growth rate shown is that between 2000 and 2015, based on the nominal dollar value of CAREC 9 imports and exports (excluding the PRC).

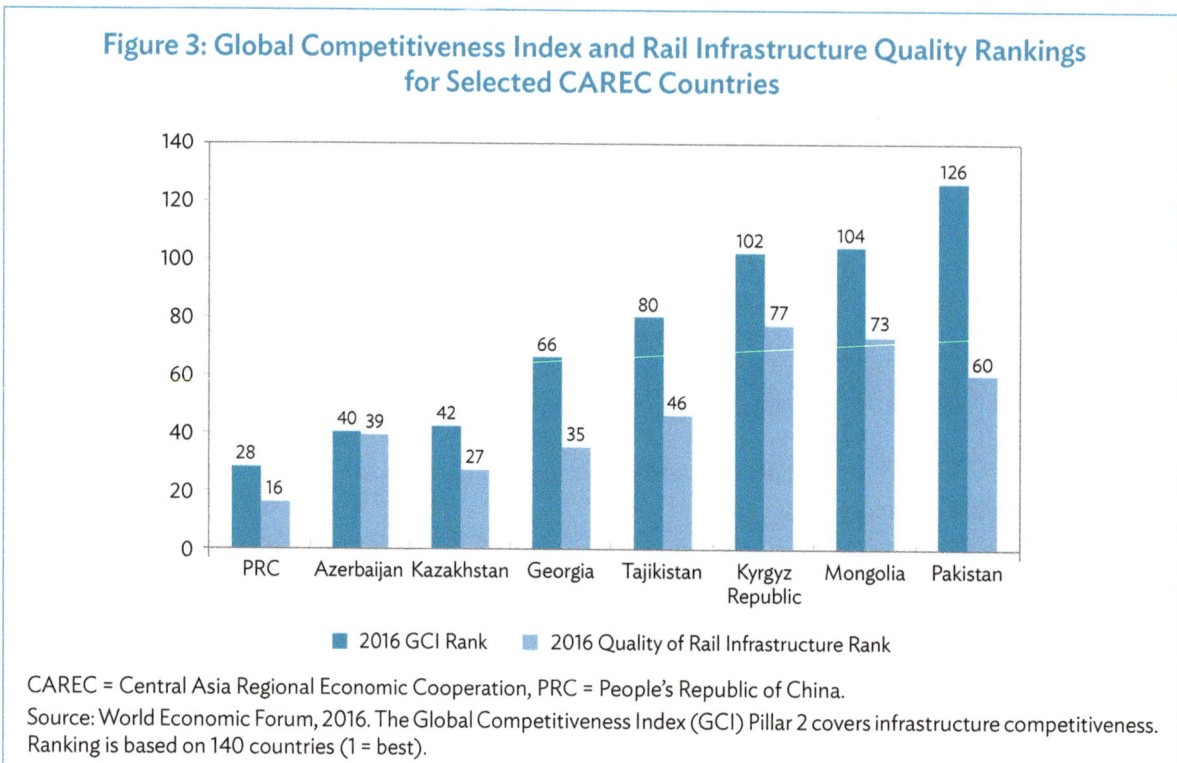

Figure 3: Global Competitiveness Index and Rail Infrastructure Quality Rankings for Selected CAREC Countries

CAREC = Central Asia Regional Economic Cooperation, PRC = People's Republic of China.
Source: World Economic Forum, 2016. The Global Competitiveness Index (GCI) Pillar 2 covers infrastructure competitiveness. Ranking is based on 140 countries (1 = best).

relatively higher ranking (less than 30). Increased competitiveness for the region depends on high quality and efficient transport infrastructure. Improvements in railway infrastructure will enhance global competitiveness and economic development. Also, improved railway infrastructure will facilitate regional cooperation and integration, providing improved connectivity between and among people, goods and services.

12. In the future, transport systems must not only be economically efficient, they must also meet new needs and expectations from users and societies. At the Paris climate conference (COP21) in December 2015, 195 countries including all 11 CAREC member countries signed the first universal climate agreement. The agreement sets out a global action plan to put the world on track to avoid dangerous climate change by limiting global warming to well below two degrees Celsius. The agreement is due to enter into force in 2020. Transport is responsible for about a quarter of the carbon dioxide emissions, and 13% of all greenhouse gases. The greenhouse gas emissions per ton-kilometer (km) for a freight train can be less than 30% of those of trucks and passenger train emissions per passenger-kilometer are less than 40% of those for passenger cars.[5] Increased use of rail transport can therefore help reduce harmful emissions.

---

[5] UIC/CER, Railway Transport and Environment – Facts & Figures.

CHAPTER 2
CAREC Railway Assessment

Considerable Infrastructure Needs

13. Most of the CAREC countries inherited railway infrastructure that is not ideally suited to their needs today. There are limitations in network design, condition, and quality. All the countries recognize the need to improve rail links with their main internal and external markets. (The current rail infrastructure situation in CAREC countries is indicated in Appendix 2.)

14. For CAREC countries, excluding the PRC, freight traffic grew at an annual rate of 3.1% from 2006 to 2012, but growth has stalled since then.[6] Increased regional and extra-regional trade can provide railways with new opportunities to earn revenues from transit traffic, an additional incentive to raise the standard of railway services.

15. Rail infrastructure investment needs in the region are considerable. It has been estimated that fast-growing middle-income countries need to spend approximately 2%–3% of gross domestic product (GDP) for development and maintenance of existing assets in the transport sector. The list of priority railway projects (Appendix 4) indicates long-term investment needs of some $38 billion on the 'core' railway network. Yet few countries in the region are or can invest at these levels.

16. There are also considerable recurrent expenditure needs in addition to the investment required to construct new infrastructure and upgrade existing routes. This includes addressing maintenance backlogs, which have accumulated over time in some member countries, and preventing further deterioration of railway assets.

17. While limitations in infrastructure cause some bottlenecks along CAREC transport routes, commercial limitations, political conflicts, and inefficient institutional arrangements create bottlenecks, too, making transit trade more difficult. These also need to be addressed for the rail sector to achieve its potential and attract new trade flows, enabling regional economic growth.

Constraints on Public Finance for Railways

18. In most CAREC countries, the public sector is the main source of funding for transport infrastructure projects and the status of such financing has been constrained in the past and may become more constrained in the current economic environment. Nearly all countries face limitations in current spending, leading to under-spending on maintenance, and adding to existing maintenance backlogs. Most CAREC countries face constraints in their ability to finance major rail investments. With limited public resources, little room exists for the public sector on its own to cope with all the investment financing needs of the railway sector.

19. These constraints have encouraged many governments to begin to reform their railways with

---

[6] Based on World Bank data for railways: goods transported (measured in millions of ton-kilometers), http://databank.worldbank.org

the objective of making them more efficient and commercially sustainable and providing a path for private investment in the sector. But such sector reform is a lengthy and difficult process.

Key Railway Reform Experience

20. In many parts of the world, railways have traditionally been government units—departments, ministries, or agencies with responsibility for self-regulation, and with a specific mandate to provide social services and internally cross-subsidize public services from bulk freight movements. As the shift occurred toward market based economies, railways increasingly struggled to keep up with the rapidly changing logistics needs of their customers. Many railways suffered a substantial decline in market share compared with other transport modes, especially compared to road transport. Governments began rail sector reforms to improve the sustainability of their rail systems and to make them more responsive to market needs. Typical reform program objectives are to:

(i) improve sustainability, safety, access, and the quality of the railway system;
(ii) reduce the economic costs of freight and passenger transport;
(iii) facilitate private investment in railway development, and, sometimes
(iv) introduce competition in railway transport.

21. Worldwide experience shows that rail sector reform efforts are challenging and take many years to implement. In the European Union (EU), rail sector reforms continue some 25 years after the first EU directive (91/440) took aim at liberalization of the sector to improve its efficiency and effectiveness. In the PRC, rail sector reforms, supported by massive government investments, have also aimed to improve the effectiveness and efficiency. The Russian Federation's rail sector reforms started in 1998 with the separation of social services and privatization of some rail supply industries. Rail reforms in the Russian Federation gathered pace in 2001 with a decree on railway reforms which set the stage for the separation of rail sector regulatory and commercial functions and the formation of the Joint Stock Company Russian Railways (JSC RZD) in 2003. The reforms continue to this day as the Joint Stock Company Russian Railways struggles with infrastructure investment needs across the vast area of the Russian Federation. In Kazakhstan, rail sector reforms, underway for more than a decade, have had a similar aim—to improve the effectiveness of the sector in the face of changing economic conditions (see Box 1).

Lessons from Experience with Railway Reforms

22. The major lessons from international experience with railway reforms and implications for CAREC countries are as follows:[7]

(i) Railways are complex industries and reform is **a long-term process**. Time and a great deal of effort are needed to put in place the necessary legislation, and institutional and commercial management structures to reform railways.
(ii) Railway reform is **a means to an end**. An initial phase of reform is often separating commercial railway functions from government regulatory and policy functions, usually forming a state-owned enterprise from railway infrastructure and operating functions and moving regulatory and policy functions into a government agency or ministry. Such a step does not, by itself, improve business performance. The business and management culture must change in both the railway enterprise and the government regulator to achieve the desired objectives. Emphasis must be placed on change management, in

---

[7] For a more complete description, refer to: Paul Amos, "Reform, Commercialization and Private Sector Participation in Railways in Eastern Europe and Central Asia," January 2005. Also see the Railway Reform Toolkit, available in several languages, including Russian, at http://www.ppiaf.org/sites/ppiaf.org/files/documents/toolkits/railways_toolkit/index.html

> **Box 1: Railway Reform in Kazakhstan**
>
> Kazakhstan's rail sector reform program started in 1997 with a resolution to merge three railway departments (Almaty, West Kazakhstan, and Tselinia railway administrations) into an integrated national railway organization, forming Kazakhstan Temir Zholy (KTZ). Reforms continued with the separation of social services (schools, hospitals, farms, and rest resorts). The aim was to integrate the three railways and to improve the efficiency and effectiveness of railway operations within the country. Internal reorganizations consolidated operations and departmental functions. In 2001, the government developed a strategy to extend the reforms with the major goals to:
>
> - Adapt the rail sector to the requirements of a market economy while maintaining government control and ownership of the railway infrastructure network;
> - Provide accessible, efficient, safe, and high quality railway services through the development of competition in rail transport and auxiliary services;
> - Create an institutional environment to attract private investment and initiative into the sector; and to develop a domestic railway supply industry.
>
> In March 2002, the national railway organization was converted into a closed joint stock company; then in 2004, it was registered as a joint stock company, Kazakhstan Temir Zholy National Company. The company was able to issue its first Euro Bond financing in 2006. In the reform process, private ownership of freight wagons was encouraged by tariff reforms and private operation of some passenger services was initiated. An integral part of the reforms was that policy and regulatory functions were separated from commercial functions, and passenger and freight activities were put in separate enterprises.
>
> As rail reforms in Kazakhstan have continued, the government has assigned additional assets to JSC KTZ, including 11 airports and three international trade zones. More progress is needed in the areas of regulatory and tariff reforms, introducing effective public service obligation contracts for passenger services, continually improving railway financial performance, generating the funds necessary for investment in upgrading the network and railway technology, liberalizing the provision of locomotives, creating competition in the passenger sector and creating an effective enabling environment for private sector investment in more areas (for example, ownership and operation of locomotives; full freight carriers; passenger operations and partial privatization).
>
> JSC KTZ = Joint Stock Company Kazakhstan Temir Zholy.
> Source: CAREC Secretariat.

the enterprise shifting from command structures to new commercially oriented structures; and in new government regulatory systems. These changes require attracting market-focused skills and experience from inside and outside the industry.

(iii) **No reform model fits all railways**. Rather, reforms need to be adopted to fit local circumstances and sensitivities. For example, restructuring small low-density railways into even smaller infrastructure and operating units is probably not an appropriate reform model, and in that case, reform emphasis is probably better placed on reforms promoting commercialization, better marketing, and improving operating efficiency.

(iv) Governments have an important role to play in the railway reform process. They must ensure **good governance and supervision** in the railway sector, set challenging targets in business plans, monitor achievements and hold management accountable for performance.

(v) There is a need for **more private sector participation** in the railway sector. Private sector participation will most likely be in rail freight asset ownership and operation. Most countries in the region will continue to own the railway infrastructure network and have social and political interests related to passenger services. Private sector entry into passenger services is also a good possibility if there is a clear mechanism to subsidize loss-making services to offset the financial impact of below cost, regulated passenger fares.

23. In most cases, the introduction of new skills into the railway sector, particularly in the design of railway freight service packages (not just raw transport) benefits from and is enhanced by adding skills from outside the rail sector, particularly from younger generation managers and specialists who are familiar with logistics concepts and with the needs of shippers.

Public Sector Support for Railway Reform

24. To be successful, railway reforms need active government support and public acceptance. Railway reform does not necessarily mean striving for stand-alone enterprise profitability. Railways with modest levels of traffic intensity and significant passenger operations will require continuing government support. Public ownership and operation of national railway networks is a legitimate public policy choice that has been made by many governments around the world. Most railway reform measures in the near term are likely to involve commercialization of lines-of-business under state-ownership, implementation of better business processes, accounting and financial management changes, better investment planning, and labor restructuring. Major reductions in the size of the networks are unlikely. There will be a continued need for public funding of the railway sector.

25. Overall, markets change over time and railways will, in the future, face further competition from other modes. Railway reforms must try to create a commercially sensitive industry that can adapt to market changes and be competitive with other modes without constant policy intervention.

Making Good Reform Decisions for Long-term Effects

26. A rail sector reform program must be set out in a clear direction but also must be implemented flexibly. Because of the strategic importance of the railway sector, governments typically adopt a cautious, long-term approach to rail sector reform efforts to help manage risk and avoid major economic shocks. However, both government reformers and policy makers must be willing to make changes as market conditions vary and other institutional sector changes evolve in the region.

CHAPTER 3
A Railway Strategy for CAREC

Vision: CAREC Railways to Become the Transport Mode of Choice by 2030

27. The CAREC strategic vision for rail transport is that rail transport will be a mode of choice for trade: quick, efficient, accessible for customers, and easy to use throughout the region by 2030. The principal approaches to achieve this vision include (i) improving rail and multimodal infrastructure; and (ii) commercializing and reforming railway activities. For the multimodal services, it is important to coordinate at the planning stage with other transport sectors such as road. When infrastructure investments and reform and commercialization components are combined as a policy package, the synergies result in rail services that are more attractive and desirable and rail transport shares will increase.

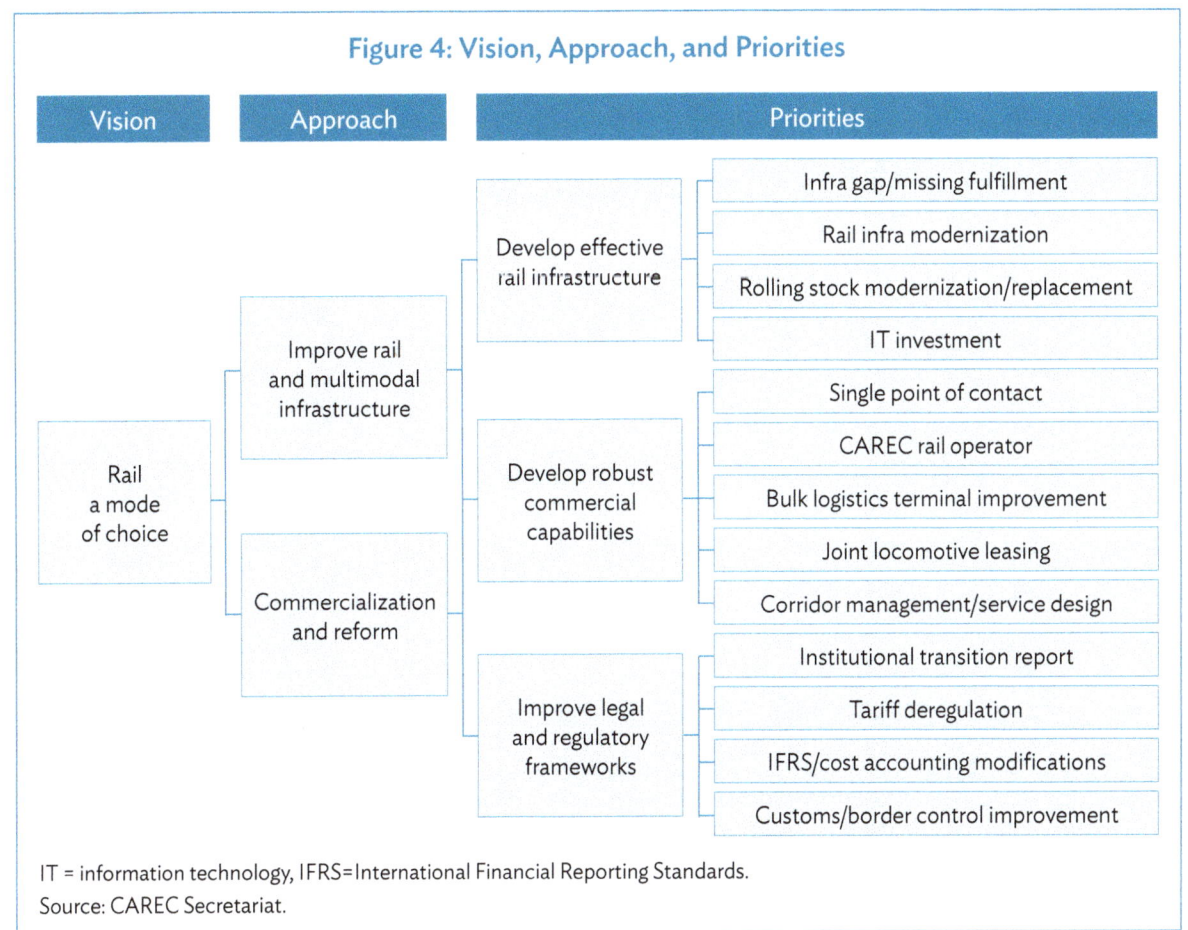

Figure 4: Vision, Approach, and Priorities

IT = information technology, IFRS = International Financial Reporting Standards.
Source: CAREC Secretariat.

Priorities

28. The priorities are based on three main components: (i) developing effective rail infrastructure; (ii) developing robust commercial capabilities; and (iii) improving legal and regulatory frameworks. The development of effective rail infrastructure may include:

(i) Filling infrastructure gaps and missing links along designated rail corridors (DRCs);
(ii) Enhancing modernization of existing infrastructure with investments such as track strengthening to increase axle-loads, train lengths, rehabilitation, electrification, and signalization;
(iii) Modernizing and replacing rolling stock to increase service capabilities, improve operational efficiency and reduce environmental impacts; and
(iv) Investing in information technology (IT) for better user orientation and efficient railway operation/maintenance.

29. The development of more robust and responsive commercial capabilities may include such options as creating a single point of contact for all shipping needs, formation of a CAREC rail operator, private investment in bulk and logistics terminals, formation of a joint locomotive leasing enterprise serving countries in the region, and development of a joint transport service design bureau. Those options, which are described in the next section, will enhance customer accessibility, while increasing the competitiveness and efficiency of railway services.

30. The improvement of legal and regulatory frameworks includes institutional transition support, tariff deregulation, implementation of international financial reporting standards (IFRS) and modern cost accounting systems which are consistent across the region, and customs and border control improvements. Such changes can facilitate investments, implementation of new commercial structures, and development of other measures that help move the rail sector toward more responsive and sustainable structures. The results-based framework of the Strategy is indicated in Appendix 1.

CHAPTER 4
Preliminary Action Plan

Effective Infrastructure Investments

31. Infrastructure investments can contribute to increasing rail market shares by improving network connectivity, increasing speeds, improving reliability, and providing additional capacity. Priority rail infrastructure investments can be put into four categories:

(i) infrastructure gap and missing link fulfillment;
(ii) rail infrastructure renovation;
(iii) rolling stock modernization and replacement; and
(iv) information technology (IT) investments.

32. Bulk and logistic terminal improvement are also increasingly important investments to better serve specialized markets, these are discussed in the commercialization or reform component. To help prioritize the infrastructure investments and service improvement, the Strategy includes designated rail corridors (DRCs), as well as a methodology for prioritizing investment projects across the region.

Infrastructure Gaps and Missing Links—Improving Network Connectivity

33. Out of the total length of 32,400 kilometers (km) of CAREC DRCs, the existing railway length is 25,200 km, i.e., 7,200 km are yet to be constructed. Examples of infrastructure investment needs may include the development of international freight corridors for mineral and oil trade, for transport of agricultural goods, connections between industrialized areas and the markets, and port-to-hinterland connections, etc.

Rail Infrastructure Modernization

34. Most CAREC railway networks were built in the distant past and some lines suffer from a lack of adequate maintenance, or have capacity limitations because of changes in traffic flows. Rail infrastructure modernization includes such investments as strengthening rail lines for higher axle loads, rehabilitation of railway lines, building and extending passing loops and bypasses, double-tracking, electrification, and signalization. Among the CAREC DRCs, 7,000 km (22%) are double track, while 3,900 km (12%) are electrified. If new traffic flows warrant, new investments to increase capacity may be a priority. In the current CAREC investment project list, there are approximately 2,000 km of proposed new railway electrification projects. For routes with heavier traffic, now or in the future, rail infrastructure renovation can be an effective and efficient investment to increase speed,[8] capacity, and reliability, and to reduce environmental impacts.

Rolling Stock Modernization/Replacement

35. In the CAREC 9 countries, there are about 3,400 locomotives; 199,500 wagons; and 6,800 coaches.[9] However, some rolling stock is old and near retirement age. In many CAREC 9 countries, there is a need to replace existing rolling stock to enhance operational capacity, reliability, and efficiency. Especially where modern electrification is proposed, existing locomotives and integrated passenger trains

---

[8] According to the CAREC Corridor Performance Measurement and Monitoring, the average commercial speed of selected rail corridors is 38.3 km per hour in 2015, increased from 27.2 km per hour in 2010 (a speed without delay basis).

[9] Based on the information provided by members of the CAREC Railway Working Group.

such as diesel multiple units and electric multiple units must be replaced.

Railway Information Technology Investments

36. Reflecting recent IT developments, IT investments to increase user orientation and to provide efficient rail operation should have a high priority. Examples of such technologies are fiber optic networks, new digital radio systems, wagon identification systems (e.g., radio-frequency identification tags) including readers/sensors, better information sharing capabilities, weight-in-motion scales along critical sections, on-board computers to enhance locomotive reporting, tractive effort, and efficiency, and electronic transmission of customs documentation. CAREC railways should nominate technical systems that will enhance regional cooperation, reduce costs, and improve railway services.

Designated Rail Corridor Investments

37. The TTFS2020 introduced the DRC concept, where long-distance freight and specific passenger services will be given priority to move through the rail system with minimal delay.[10] The Strategy selected DRCs by renaming and refining the proposed DRCs in the TTFS 2020 to reflect the current situation (Map 1). The purposes of selecting DRCs are to prioritize infrastructure projects (IP) on the corridors; and to conduct soft policies such as trial runs of trains and tariff agreements by some countries on the corridors. The selection criteria for DRCs include carrying significant volumes of international rail traffic (present and future); and strategic or geopolitical considerations such as enhancing intermodal linkages and port–hinterland connections. The same six main corridors, which were defined in TTFS 2020 as multimodal corridors, have been also used for the definition of the six refined DRC corridors. It is noted that DRC 3 and 6 include connections between Europe/Russian Federation and Iran through some of the CAREC countries given the importance of connections to the Arabian Sea. A detailed description of each DRC is given in Appendix 3.

Action Plan Items:

38. To develop corridor investments and help prioritize them, more due diligence will be needed. This should include feasibility level estimates of costs, analysis of markets served and traffic impacts, analysis of parties who benefit, analysis of financial and economic returns, and a discussion of financing mechanisms, including alternative and structured finance. Especially, it is important to conduct a traffic forecast based on reliable data and marketing studies to increase the demand from the multimodal context.

Prioritization Methodology

39. Evaluating and prioritizing infrastructure projects require intensive discussions involving many stakeholders: economists, companies, politicians, civilians, town and country planners, authorities, ecologists, and bankers. All have something to contribute, and sometimes have conflicting views and interests. For this reason, it is essential to develop a transparent evaluation and prioritization methodology, including traffic model analysis.

40. The effects of a major infrastructure project are numerous and differ in type and character. The financial cost–benefit analysis (CBA) provides an estimate of financial impact, while an economic CBA includes the benefits to society, expressed in monetary terms. This economic CBA may include the effects of the investment on regional traffic flows as well as external benefits caused by reduced road maintenance costs, road accidents, air pollution, noise, and effects on climate change. Furthermore, to include effects that cannot be expressed in monetary terms, or are not quantified at all, multi-criteria analysis (MCA) may be added to properly evaluate project options. Appendix 5 provides an

---

[10] CAREC Transport and Trade Facilitation Strategy 2020, http://www.adb.org/sites/default/files/institutional-document/34107/files/carec-ttfs-2020.pdf

Preliminary Action Plan 13

Map 1: Central Asia Regional Economic Cooperation Designated Rail Corridors

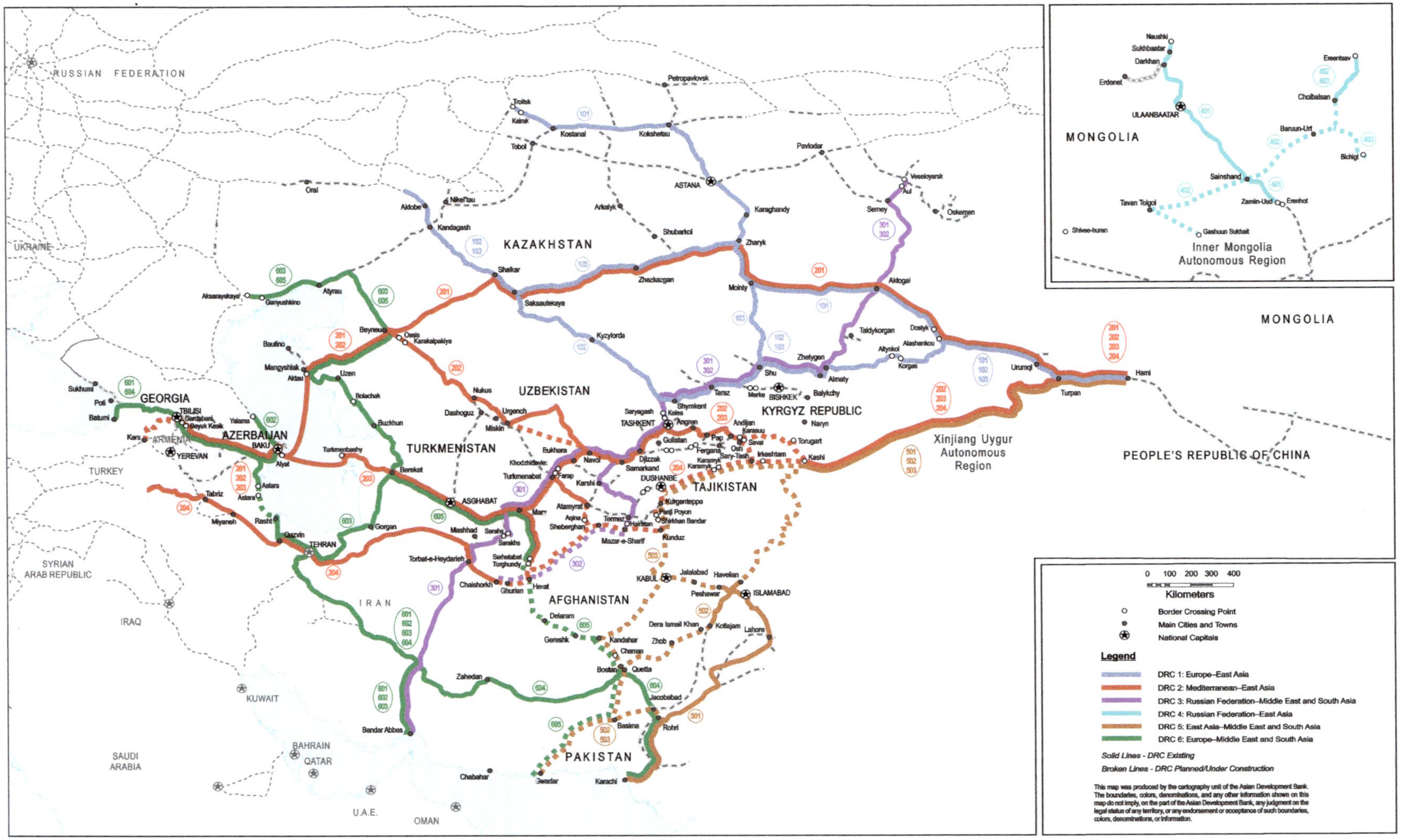

Source: CAREC Secretariat.

elaboration on rail infrastructure evaluation and prioritization methodologies.

Enhancing Interoperability

41. When considering the corridor investments, it is important to enhance the interoperability among the countries. Especially, it should be noted that there are three different rail gauge-groups in CAREC (1,435 millimeter (mm) standard gauge, used in the PRC; 1,520 mm Russian gauge, used in Commonwealth of Independent States (CIS) countries; and 1,676 mm broad gauge, used in Pakistan). Given that different fundamental technical standards are used in each group, interoperability usually focuses on standards of interchange facility design, efficient load transfers, and operational coordination of equipment and facilities. The promotion of common technical standards has been studied at such organizations as International Union of Railways (UIC) and Organization for Cooperation of Railways (OSJD).

Robust Commercial Capacity

42. A major issue for most shippers is the difficulty in conducting commercial transactions with railways for international freight movements. Such arrangements often require dealing with several railways for an array of services and providing and gathering information which includes: getting tariffs, making pre-payment arrangements with multiple railways, finding freight wagons, balancing container and wagon flows, handling customs issues, making security arrangements, checking on the progress of shipments, finding how to claim for any loss and damage, and arranging for final delivery options.

43. The development of a range of commercial responses to these complex and overlapping problems can make rail transport more comprehensible, easier to arrange, and more attractive. Several international freight logistics companies (e.g., DB Schenker, DHL, and a few others) have shown that if these issues can be solved, valuable long-distance containerized international freight shipments can be attracted to rail from other modes, including air transport. There remain significant interregional freight flows of containerized and other goods that could also move by rail but customers are often dispersed and harder to organize. There are a number of steps that can be taken to develop better commercial capacities for these interregional freight traffic flows.[11] Some are described below:

Single Point of Contact

44. While each CAREC railway has an internal freight forwarder, most international shippers consider this a burden rather than a benefit—railway freight forwarders usually offer only limited services for international shipments, and many shippers already have a commercial forwarder or logistics provider. CAREC railways could form a regional joint freight forwarding company, perhaps together with an experienced private forwarder, to offer integrated freight forwarding and logistics services across the region. The CAREC forwarder would integrate logistics services, including those of international partners, to provide a single source for customers to arrange rail movements throughout the region, and provide a single point for handling all aspects of rail movements including loading and unloading, pickup and delivery, customs and duty formalities at all border crossings, and warehousing and storage services if required. Several railways are developing international freight forwarder capabilities (e.g., KTZ Express with both DHL and DB Schenker) that could be integrated with the combined CAREC forwarder to serve customers throughout the CAREC region. These international logistics companies focus on large flows across long distances (e.g., PRC to Europe). The regional CAREC forwarder can focus on serving shorter distance but important international flows.

---

[11] To indicate the improved service level, it is important to monitor the commercial perception of railway services from the users' point of view. Also, to indicate the operational efficiency of a railway, employee productivity (e.g. output in traffic units per employee) can be monitored.

45. While there may be no restrictions on joint ownership of a commercial entity within the CAREC countries, the laws and regulations in each country should be reviewed to ensure that the new company would have full authority to contract for transport services, serve as a payment center for railway tariffs regionally, and could contract for "last-kilometer" pick-up and delivery services. A CAREC regional forwarder would have to be licensed in each country and establish offices throughout the region. This forwarder/logistics provider could develop first along individual corridors, as the participating railways reach commercial agreements between themselves. It will also be important to ensure that freight forwarder pricing is not regulated as a part of rail transport tariffs (because the joint forwarder will provide a range of services, including arranging for rail freight transport).

Action Plan Items:

46. Review legal and regulatory structures in each participating country; develop potential ownership structures, scope of services and how a CAREC forwarder would link with railways, develop a proposal for the formation of the company. Find interested railway partners along corridors or in commercial clusters serving customers in the region.

Create a Common CAREC Rail Operator

47. Most CIS countries have transport laws and leasing regulations that permit the formation and functioning of rail operators—essentially freight forwarders or logistics companies that own freight wagons. The freight forwarder discussed above as the single point of contact for customers could become a rail wagon operator, providing rail car services to any CAREC member.[12] In the past, it was difficult to privately finance railway equipment within a single country because of unfavorable tariff structures and the risks associated with having a single client railway. However, a CAREC regional common rail operator could provide freight cars and forwarding services across the CAREC region. Initially, the CAREC forwarder/operator could be owned by several individual CAREC railways, perhaps first along a corridor or among a few CAREC railways, later expanding to include other CAREC railways as needed. Using this ownership structure, an initial tranche of new wagons could be financed by the multilateral development banks. Eventually, the CAREC forwarder/operator could be sold in stages to enhance private financing opportunities.

48. Generally, the major CIS railways in the region have already separated rail tariffs into their major components (wagons, locomotives, energy, infrastructure, other). Other CAREC railways should also do this. For a rail operator to be successful, the tariff "discount" it receives for providing private wagons must be sufficient to enable it to invest in wagons and meet debt service requirements, given expected wagon utilization. In most CIS countries, prices charged for transport services by rail operators (which include forwarding services, wagon supply, the applicable rail tariff, and other service-related charges) are not regulated.

49. While there are a number of rail operator examples in several CIS countries, probably the closest model to the CAREC rail operator enterprise proposed here is the recently formed United Transport and Logistics Company (UTLC) that serves the Eurasian Economic Union (EAEU). UTLC is jointly owned by the individual railways of Kazakhstan, the Russian Federation, and Belarus. It operates 67 railway terminals and 5 border crossing points (including Khorgos, Dostyk), has 33,000 container wagons, 71,000 ISO containers, owns or operates rail ferries and trucks, and has 600 offices throughout the EAEU and 40 international offices outside the EAEU. UTLC handles mostly container services but also operates non-containerized bulk terminals. The company serves over 70,000 clients, providing a single point of contact for rail container transport. Other examples of rail operators working across country borders include EastComTrans, an

---

[12] Initially, this wagon capability may be limited to CIS rail gauge rolling stock, but it could evolve to include broad and standard gauge equipment over time.

operator of tank and semi wagons headquartered in Kazakhstan with operations into the Russian Federation.

50. A common rail operator could serve as a single point of contact for customers, as a wagon supplier throughout the region (at least in CIS gauge countries), as a terminal operator, and even provide wagon and locomotive leasing services to member railways. It would serve as an integrator of information from all CAREC railways, and define and develop commercial rail services throughout the CAREC region.

51. Multiple rail operators could be envisioned—each specializing in a corridor, or type of commodity or customer (e.g., oil and gas products), or wagon type. UTLC is an example of a regional rail operator specializing in container services. It also operates terminals. The development of a common rail operator could start with several interested countries operating along a corridor and later expand as other CAREC railways wished to join.

Action Plan Items:

52. Determine the level of interest in a CAREC rail operator among CAREC members, review legal and regulatory structures in each participating country (e.g., examine whether tariffs are adequately remunerative for private wagon operators, review empty movement costs), develop potential ownership structures, determine if the common rail operator can subsume the role of the common freight forwarder, develop an initial wagon acquisition program based on the needs of member railways, and conduct due diligence, including development of financial structures.

Establish Bulk and Logistics Terminals

53. Many rail movements can benefit from consolidation in bulk and logistics terminals. Bulk terminals can service commodities such as fertilizers, chemicals, refined petroleum products, cement and aggregates, and various minerals where concentration of multiple shipments into a single-movement block train can reduce transport costs, improve wagon utilization, offer more customized services, and more frequent service schedules to customers. The CAREC railways (and major customers) can help to develop high-volume bulk distribution and logistics terminals (for consolidation and de-consolidation). A plan for the development of bulk distribution and logistics terminals would be needed and an ownership structure for the facilities discussed among major shippers, forwarders, and railway entities. At gauge change locations, bulk distribution terminals could also provide trans-loading capabilities.

Action Plan Items:

54. Determine interest across CAREC railways for these types of terminals; conduct market and customer research into demand and potential pricing structures; develop proposed transport services (service designs including service routes, train size, frequencies); determine interest of multiple parties (including forwarders, shippers, shipper associations, local governments, railways); conduct due diligence to develop ownership structures, pricing, investment needs, and consider alternative financing arrangements.

Promote Joint Locomotive Leasing

55. Since the common rail operator should be able to enter into transactions with shippers and railways in any member country, it would be possible for it to acquire locomotives that could be used on any CIS-gauge CAREC-member railway. As with wagons, the fact that there are multiple customers (the national railways) mitigates the risk associated with financing locomotives for a single national railway. This should permit locomotives to be privately financed, as long as the technical specifications of the locomotives are sufficiently common. Given that CAREC CIS members use similar technical standards, it should be possible for a leasing company to provide locomotives throughout CAREC's Russian-gauge subregion. CAREC rail operator locomotives could be provided on a short-term or long-term lease basis to any CIS CAREC member.

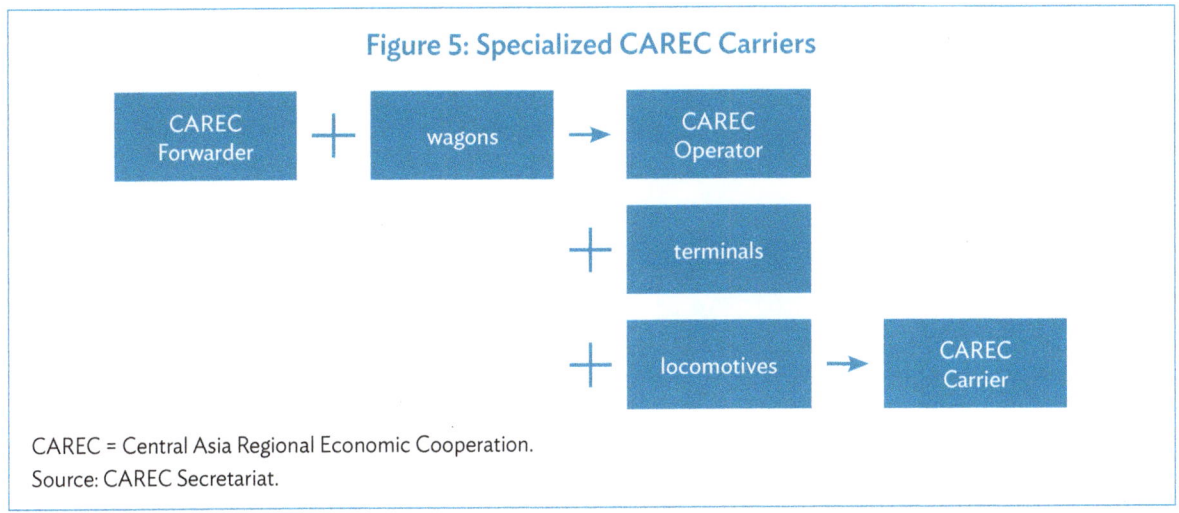

Figure 5: Specialized CAREC Carriers

CAREC = Central Asia Regional Economic Cooperation.
Source: CAREC Secretariat.

56. Eventually, if institutional and legal reforms permit the operation of independent rail carriers, the CAREC rail operator could become a specialized regional rail carrier, providing wagons, locomotives, and customer services (including logistics services) to customers throughout the region.

Action Plan Items:

57. As with wagon investments, determine interest; review legal and regulatory structures; develop potential ownership structures; develop an initial estimate of the types and quantity of locomotives that would be acquired, along with some indicative leasing arrangements; and conduct due diligence of the proposed structure and investments, including alternative financing arrangements.

Create Specialized CAREC Carriers

58. It is possible to speculate the creation of a specialized CAREC rail carrier evolving from entities which can own and operate wagons, terminals, and lease locomotives in the CAREC region (Figure 5). This entity would have customer relationships, and plan and operate trains between its terminals and for movement into and from the CAREC network. A CAREC carrier would rely on individual railways to provide dispatching, communications, and drivers for the trains. Alternatives could include having the CAREC locomotive entity lease locomotives to the railway and use these locomotives to move CAREC rail operator trains. At some point the distinction becomes hard to define. The development of such specialized carriers will depend on the legal and regulatory structure in each country and the level of interest of individual CAREC railways.

Action Plan Items:

59. Determine interest; review legal and regulatory structures; develop potential ownership structures; determine relationships with CAREC railways; conduct due-diligence of the proposed structure and investments, including alternative financing arrangements; and develop an implementation plan.

CAREC Corridor Management and Service Design

60. Railways are most effective operating block trains between major terminal points. Most national railways develop service designs (train schedules and what traffic trains will carry) by considering internal operational needs, including costs, equipment utilization, and service requirements. For CAREC's international movements a new transport service design entity could be created to develop coordinated movements between railways, to ensure that international movements receive consideration in individual railway service designs, to optimize rolling stock use, and to operationally monitor train services (Figure 6). This unit would work with CAREC

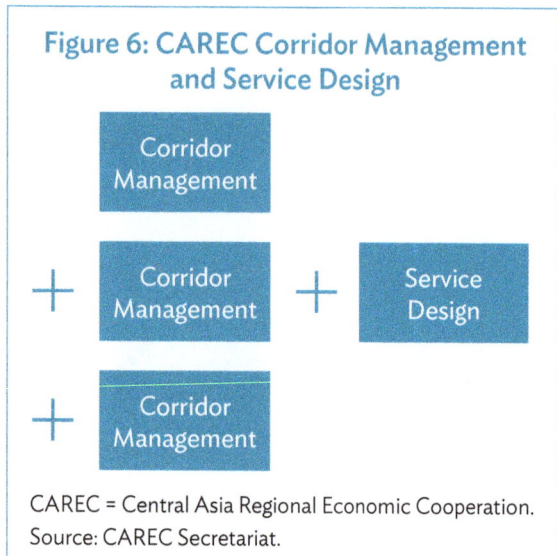

Figure 6: CAREC Corridor Management and Service Design

CAREC = Central Asia Regional Economic Cooperation.
Source: CAREC Secretariat.

rail operators and rely on corridor management units to provide a CAREC wide service.

61. To improve operations along a corridor and allow the integration of international and domestic traffic in trains, CAREC railways may wish to develop a corridor management and service design unit for busy corridors. The duties and responsibilities of a corridor management unit could be expanded to include interaction with CAREC railway dispatching activities, and to communicate the availability of regional trains and determine CAREC railway service performance on a day-to-day basis. The unit could also interact with common rail operators and with customers, informing them of changes and dealing with customer inquiries about service.

62. Eventually, in order to increase interregional coordination, the service design unit may function across the region and CAREC rail operators that may be specialized by commodity and corridor.

Action Plan Items:

63. Determine interest among CAREC railways; define functions, responsibilities, and relationships with CAREC railways; develop agreement from CAREC railways to share movement and train dispatch information; develop communications requirements and the location of the corridor management and service design functions; conduct legal and regulatory due diligence; define proposed structures by country and any investments necessary; and develop implementation plan.

Railway Efficiency and Cost Reduction

64. Many elements of the CAREC rail strategy will depend upon and affect the efficiency and operating practices of member railways. Some of the strategic investment initiatives—not only new lines, but also the implementation of modern technologies (signals, fiber optics, electrification, to name a few)—may have a significant impact on railway efficiency and result in a reduction in costs for member railways. Another source of cost reductions may involve changes in land use, employment, employee training needs, and similar adjustments. CAREC railways may seek technical and financial support to help achieve such potential efficiencies and cost reductions.

Action Plan Items:

65. Efficiency and cost reduction analysis will be part of most strategic infrastructure investments.[13] Efficiency, employment, cost reduction and social impact analyses should be included as a part of the implementation due diligence for all strategic initiatives. Financial assistance might be obtained from the multilateral development banks.

Land Management and Real Estate Development

66. Most CAREC railways have a large endowment of land and related facilities, some of which may no longer be needed because of changes in traffic patterns or due to construction of new lines. Some of this land may be commercially valuable for

---

[13] One of the indicators to monitor the operation efficiency of the railway agency is the working ratios (expenses without depreciation/revenue).

the development of new railway traffic (e.g., land provided for the development of a bulk distribution terminal, or for a new factory). Ownership and development rights for railway land are often not clearly specified in existing laws and regulations. Such issues should be included in the legal and regulatory review discussed above. In addition, many railways may not have sufficient real estate expertise to properly develop land and handle leasing or title transfer. These issues should be addressed as part of each strategic initiative and may also be addressed in the institutional and regulatory reform tasks.

Action Plan Items:

67. Management of land and real estate development are important skills for railway management. Development or acquisition of these skills should be included as a part of the implementation due diligence for all strategic initiatives. Financial assistance to improve efficiency and reduce cost might be obtained from multilateral development banks.

Institutional, Legal, and Regulatory Initiatives

68. Railways across the CAREC region are organized in many different ways—some as government departments, some with their own railway ministry, and several have restructured the national railway into a state-owned company (some as closed and others as open joint stock companies). Often, many different laws define and regulate various components of the rail sector. In some countries, only railway infrastructure is part of the monopoly sector; in others, the entire sector is considered a 'natural monopoly' (a distinct type of monopoly that may arise when there are extremely high fixed costs of distribution, such as exist when large-scale infrastructure is required to ensure supply). The formation of the EAEU imposes legal constraints on some CAREC railways, while others, not a part of the EAEU, have different constraints. As a part of continuing evolution of economic development in CAREC countries, some governments may wish to transition the legal framework of their national railways from one form to another. Transition support is traditionally a part of multilateral development bank assistance and should be available for CAREC countries wishing to investigate and implement these types of structural changes.

69. This complex set of legal and regulatory constraints may affect implementation of some of the strategic initiatives, including some of the alternative financing structures. A set of institutional, legal and regulatory initiatives is included in the Strategy, to be used when desired or needed.

Institutional Transition Support

70. This initiative will support governments wishing to implement changes in the institutional structure of their rail sector. In each case, governments could request transition support from multilateral development banks and transition support services discussed on an individual basis. The banks have a great deal of experience to offer in supporting institutional changes in the rail sector and possess a body of knowledge that governments can draw on to inform the transition process.

Action Plan Items:

71. Governments seeking advice and support on rail sector transition should discuss their needs and intentions with the multilateral development banks so that a customized set of support services can be discussed, designed, and taken up if desired upon request.

Tariff and Pricing Regulations

72. Most countries regulate prices or tariffs in natural monopoly sectors. In some CIS countries such regulation has opened a path to private ownership of some railway assets (e.g., freight wagons, locomotives, loading and unloading facilities). Some international tariffs may discourage trade; others may be insufficient to allow railways to finance important investments. A comparative study of international tariffs by major commodity applicable to international trade (import, export,

and transit), and allowances made in the tariffs for private investment, may reveal instances where tariff charge could help to increase market share and attract private investment.

73. All countries allow the operation of both railway and private freight forwarders but not all allow operations by private international wagon operators. Typically, while most components of the railway tariff are regulated, prices charged to customers by wagon operators (either state-owned or private) are not. Private wagon operators are commercial enterprises and depend on providing profitable services to attract investment and sustainable fund operations. Railways can attract private investment if there is sufficient room in the market place for rail operators (or specialized carriers) to invest and fund operations.

74. In addition to national regulations, international railway tariffs are usually governed by a long-established set of institutions, procedures, and agreements which may make changing tariffs difficult. If international railway trade is to be sustainable and responsive to changes in the competitive environment, railways must be able to modify the prices they charge for transport services, sometimes on specific traffics and routes.[14] Implementation of some customer related initiatives (e.g., a single point of contact forwarder, CAREC rail operators, specialized rail operators with distribution facilities, CAREC carriers) may require more railway pricing flexibility than is now permitted. Improved responsibility and location based cost accounting systems may also show that some current tariffs are un-remunerative for rail carriers.

75. Tariff and rail service pricing regulations should be reviewed with a view to permitting a wider range of private investment and asset ownership structures. Where it is found that rail costs are out of line with the competitive market price, methods to reduce railway costs and investments or to enhance service must be found.

Action Plan Items:

76. CAREC member's advice on tariff and pricing regulations should be sought. Railways wishing to implement more flexible tariffs can request legal and regulatory support for determining the changes that might be needed to increase tariff flexibility and to permit the implementation of increased private sector investment. Railways and governments seeking advice and support on rail sector pricing practices, including bilateral tariff agreement, should discuss their interests and intentions with the multilateral development banks so that a customized set of support services can be discussed, designed, and taken up if needed.

Implementation of IFRS and Cost Accounting Modifications

77. Separation of accounts between passenger, freight, rolling stock, and infrastructure services is an important part of developing a competitive rail freight industry. Development of refined and modern cost accounting systems, including accounting separation, is crucial to achieve the transparency required to define and manage different rail markets. It is common in CAREC countries for railway freight services to cross-subsidize passenger services. While this may be government policy, without adequate cost accounting systems, it is impossible to measure the extent or cost of such cross-subsidies. If specialized CAREC carriers or rail operators are to evolve, railways must ensure that government subsidy, embedded cross-subsidy, and pricing regulations are realistic and well understood.

78. To participate in alternative financing structures, including joint ownership structures, railways will need to implement international financial reporting standards. IFRS accounting practices should be implemented in conjunction with the development of improved cost accounting systems which are as consistent as possible across systems.

---

[14] Some EAEU railways have the ability to vary tariffs on specific traffics and commodities within a limited range and subject to certain competitive and cost recovery considerations.

Action Plan Items:

79. Governments and railways seeking advice and support for the development of IFRS accounting and improved cost accounting standards should discuss their desires and intentions with the multilateral development banks so that a customized set of support services can be discussed, designed, and taken up if needed.

Reform of Legal and Regulatory Frameworks

80. Some strategic initiatives may require modification or elaboration of national laws and regulations regarding leasing, financing, accounting standards, private ownership of rail related assets, and a myriad of other issues. Such changes and modifications are likely to be country-specific (i.e., changes needed in one country may be different than the changes needed in another country). For implementing specific strategic initiatives, the legal and regulatory framework governing railway assets, pricing, leasing, and international joint venture ownership structures in each country should be reviewed and changes recommended.

Action Plan Items:

81. Legal and regulatory due diligence must be part of an implementation plan for any strategic initiative (e.g., CAREC forwarders, CAREC wagon operators, CAREC carriers, and CAREC distribution centers). The legal and regulatory review can inform decisions about the structure of commercial units that are jointly owned by the CAREC railways and on important regulations regarding leasing, pricing, land ownership, applicable tax regimes, and other regulations that may affect implementation plans.

Customs and Border Controls

82. The intent of the Strategy is to increase the railway share of international freight transport markets in the region. Customs procedures and border controls are an important element of international railway traffic flows. As rail freight traffic shifts toward block train movements, it would be helpful to develop improved customs and border control procedures. These modern transit regimes should include electronic document transmission, development of trusted and certified forwarder/operator programs, and procedures that can eliminate border inspections and delays. The aim here would be for most railway freight trains to be pre-cleared at the point of origin, and then operate across national borders without additional inspections or delays.

Action Plan Items:

83. Multilateral development banks have a number of tools to help countries develop paperless borders. Improvements in customs and border control efficiency should be part of many strategic railway infrastructure investments and should be included as a part of the implementation of due diligence for all strategic initiatives. Assistance in financing improved customs and border controls might be obtained from the banks.

CHAPTER 5
Implementing the Strategy

84. The full implementation of the proposed actions in this Strategy requires a robust arrangement addressing money (financing), people (capacity), and technology, with distinct roles identified for railways, governments and development partners. An action plan and corresponding results-based framework has been developed, and will be subject to periodic monitoring, review and adjustments by the CAREC Railway Working Group.

Mobilize and Leverage Sufficient Financing

85. CAREC railways and governments, in considering how to finance infrastructure projects, may start by categorizing projects into those with net positive financial returns versus those with net negative financial returns. For the former grouping, the CAREC railways and governments may consider structuring the project so as to allow private financing support for the project. This is especially true for investments in rolling stock. These structures may include, special purpose vehicles with mixed ownership, public–private partnerships, operating leases, or formation of a separate enterprise and issuance of corporate bonds. Other structures are also possible. Efforts should also be made to minimize direct public subsidies by recycling user charges back to the project, capturing value uplift of surrounding land through some form of tax or fee, etc. Legal frameworks for railways to use these mechanisms must be established in each country. A certain percentage of taxes/levies charged on road transport may also be used to support railways, on grounds of correcting for the negative externalities of road transport such as congestion, accidents, or wear and tear on the road network, which can be alleviated by traffic shifting to railways.

86. Financing mechanisms, and financial structuring models, should be developed and reviewed by CAREC governments and other entities to ensure they are compatible with the legal, regulatory and political context of each country. To this end, CAREC countries, supported by development partners, may conduct research into alternative financing structures and mechanisms applicable to investments in railway assets, and

---

Box 2: Alternative Financing Mechanisms for Railway Development in the People's Republic of China

The recent World Bank report, entitled "Attracting Capital for Railway Development in the PRC," provides 15 case studies about how rail organizations in the PRC and seven other countries have attracted capital and made capital budgeting decisions to support their strategic development.

The study suggests that China Railway Corporation can (i) expand its financial sources through organizing and managing its subsidiary entities to maximize their value and generation of cash flows; (ii) effectively apply public–private partnership concepts through land value capture and integrated land development; (iii) capture its right-of-way value through telecommunications services; (iv) raise new equity through initial public offerings of profitable and well governed subsidiary entities; and (v) leverage financing from the railway's large fixed asset base.

The report concludes that railways worldwide have been able to employ a wide range of mechanisms to attract investment capital. A common requirement for the investor is that the investment is profitable and the profit is commensurate with the risks undertaken.

Source: The World Bank: http://www.worldbank.org/en/news/press-release/2016/03/11/alternative-financing-mechanisms-for-railway-development-in-china

develop a menu of potentially useful financing mechanisms with an explanation of how and when they might be used.

Building Capacity

87. Implementation of the Strategy requires CAREC governments and railways to obtain and maintain knowledge on all the operational priorities. To this end, CAREC governments and railways, supported by development partners, may:

- Conduct a needs assessment of capacity required, and prioritize the capacity building needs;
- Conduct capacity building (training) sessions at future CAREC Railway Working Group meetings on identified priorities;
- Maximize the use of partnerships with expert organizations, such as the UIC and OSJD.

88. In doing so, knowledge and expertise already existing among CAREC railways should be examined and mutually shared. Experience from outside CAREC countries should be tapped to help addressing the institutional and technical challenges in CAREC railways.

Transfer of Technology

89. Finally, CAREC railways should identify, prioritize and apply new technologies that support the vision—to make rail the transport mode of choice in the region. It is recognized that the choice of the right technology should be based on the actual needs of the operators and users of the railways.

90. CAREC development partners may support such technology transfer through (i) investment projects with components that feature new technologies, and (ii) technical assistance.

APPENDIX 1
Results-Based Framework

Impact		
Rail transport will be a mode of choice for trade: quick, efficient, accessible for customers, and easy to use throughout the region.		
Outcomes	**Outcome milestones/indicators**	**Data sources**
1. Railway's service level on main corridors improved	Average commercial speed[a] of rail transport on main designated rail corridors increased by 20% by 2030	CAREC CPMM
	Commercial perception of quality of railway infrastructure improved by each country by 2030	Global Competitiveness Index published by the World Economic Forum
2. Railway's operation efficiency improved	Railway employee productivity (annual output/employee)[b] improved by 10%	CAREC country railway agencies
Outputs	**Output milestones/indicators**	**Data sources**
1. Effective rail infrastructure developed	By 2030	
	Completed 3,000 km of new railway construction, and railway track renovation, electrification or signalization	CAREC country railway agencies
	Increased route length of multi-tracked rail lines (5% increase of total route-km)	CAREC country railway agencies
	Increased route length of electrification of rail lines (10% increase of total route-km)	CAREC country railway agencies
	At least two DRCs linking international main maritime hubs and regional logistics terminals prioritized, developed, and fully operational	CAREC country railway agencies
2. Robust commercial capabilities developed	By 2030	
	Working ratios[c] of all railways become less than 1	CAREC country railway agencies
	Regional institutional partnership established (such as CAREC joint rail operator) among the logistics and transport operators, and railway authorities	CAREC country railway agencies
	At least five bulk and logistic terminals for international traffic developed/improved	CAREC country railway agencies

continued on next page

Table *continued*

Outputs	Output milestones/indicators	Data sources
3. Legal and regulatory frameworks improved	By 2030	
	IFRS introduced in majority of CAREC countries	CAREC country railway agencies
	Effective legal and regulatory regimes developed	CAREC country railway agencies
	Bilateral tariff agreement established	CAREC country railway agencies
	Modern transit regimes designed	CAREC country railway agencies
Inputs		
	From 2017 to 2030	
	Eight feasibility studies completed/in progress by four CAREC railway agencies	Project Completion Reports
	Resources (short-term $10 billion and long-term $38 billion) provided for priority projects by multiple sources, including public, private, and a combination of the two through public–private partnerships, as well as from domestic, bilateral and international development partner sources	Country infrastructure development strategies
		Country railway development master plans
		Project appraisal reports
	New financing partnerships and nonpublic finance resources mobilized	Country Partnership Strategy and operational plans of multilateral development banks
	New innovative financing approaches mobilized (such as infrastructure bonds and guarantees) to provide additional resources	Bilateral partners and other donors
		Private sectors
	Region-wide promotion of common technical standards, tariff and costing benchmarks developed in close collaboration and coordination with UIC and OSJD and other partners	International and domestic commercial banks
	Seven technical assistance projects and capacity building activities (total value of $13.9 million) closely coordinated and implemented among national, regional, and international development organizations	

CAREC = Central Asia Regional Economic Cooperation, CPMM = Corridor Performance Measurement and Monitoring, DRC = designated rail corridor, IFRS = International financial reporting standards, OSJD = Organization for Cooperation of Railways, UIC = International Union of Railways

[a] Average travel speed of commercially operated trains.
[b] Employee productivity is annual output (in traffic units) per employee. Traffic units are the sum of passenger kilometers and freight tonne-kilometers.
[c] Operating expenses without depreciation and/or revenue.
Source: CAREC Secretariat.

APPENDIX 2
Central Asia Regional Economic Cooperation Railway Map

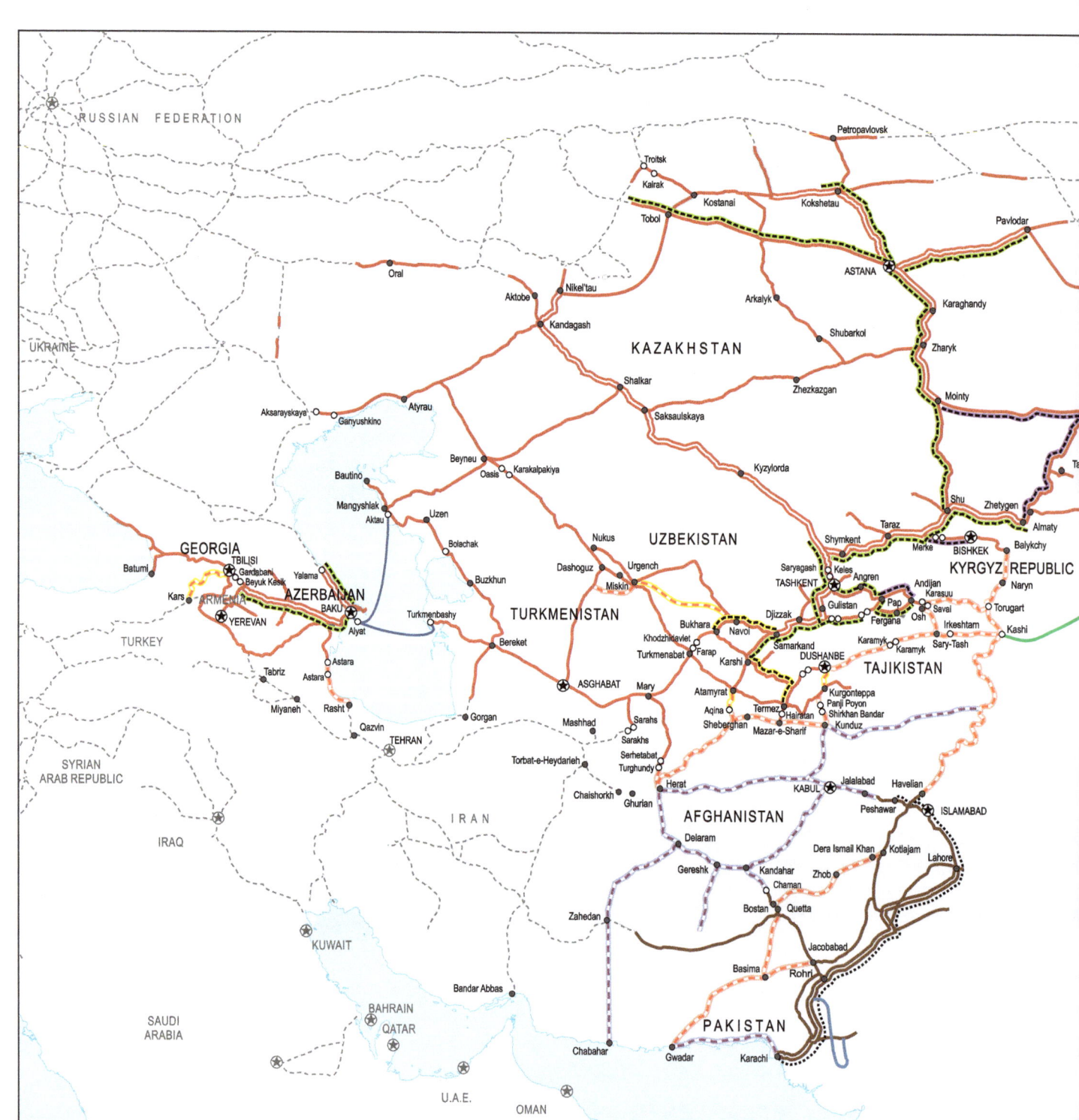

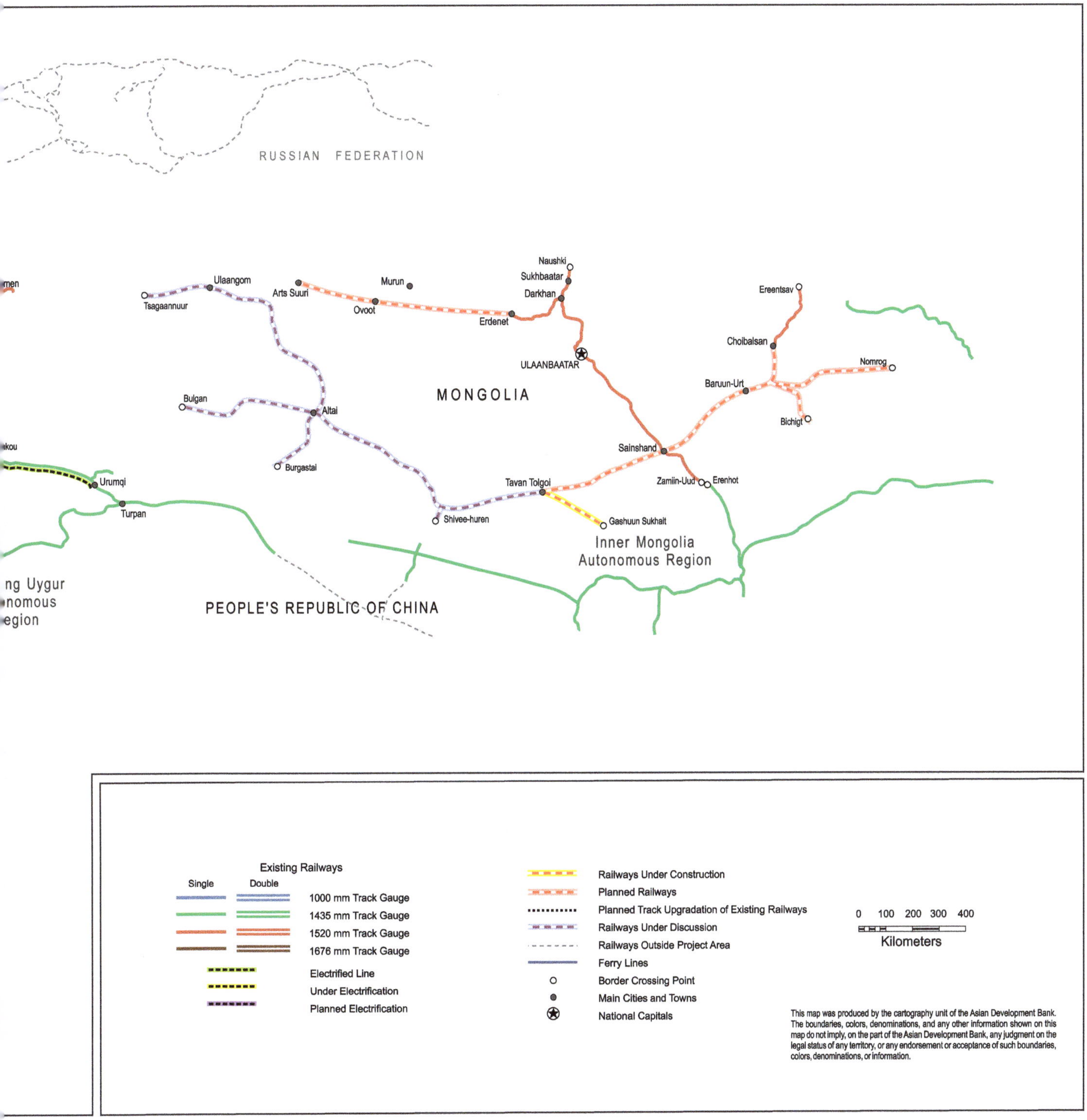

Central Asia Regional Economic Cooperation Railway Map 27

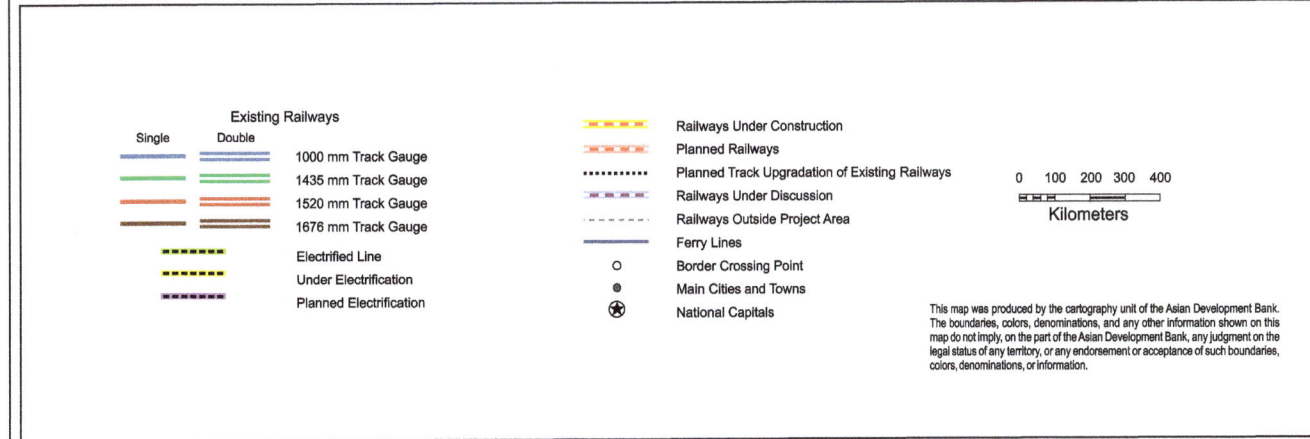

APPENDIX 3
Designated Rail Corridors[1]

DRC 1: Europe–East Asia

Given the increased volume of trade between the People's Republic of China (PRC) and Europe, DRC 1 plays a crucial role in freight rail traffic. Future growth in trade volume is also expected in line with the increasing number of container block trains between the PRC and Europe, as well as the needs of international bulk freight rail transport, such as minerals and grains. Two railway border crossing points (BCPs) between the PRC and Kazakhstan are important for DRC 1, namely: (i) Alashankou–Dostyk; and (ii) Korgas–Altynkol, mainly due to the impact of infrastructure capacity limitations and procedural inefficiencies at BCPs on the total time of transport along DRC 1. The two BCPs are also the point-of-gauge change locations (1,435 mm gauge in the PRC and 1,520 mm gauge in Kazakhstan). Three sub-corridors have been identified under DRC 1:

- **DRC 101: Hami (PRC)–Urumqi (PRC)–Alashankou (PRC)–Dostyk (KAZ)–Mointy (KAZ)–Astana (KAZ)–Kairak (KAZ)–Troisk (RUS)**

    With a total length of approximately 3,100 km, DRC 101 is characterized by heavy freight traffic volume. DRC 101 is mainly used for domestic freight transport but is also important as an international freight rail corridor that connects the PRC, the Russian Federation, and Europe. The rail corridor's technical features are more developed, with about 35% of DRC 101 electrified, and about 29% double-tracked. Although there are no missing links in DRC 101, there are plans for electrification of about 800 km in DRC 101 (KAZ IP6 and IP7). With heavy traffic volume at Alashankou–Dostyk BCP (10 million tons/year of rail traffic from Dostyk to Alashankou; and 6 million tons/year for the opposite direction), the effective use of the BCP should be a major issue. DRC 101 has many sections that are overlapping with routes identified in the Trans-Asian Railway (TAR) and the OSJD Corridors 2 and 5.

- **DRC 102: Hami (PRC)–Urumqi (PRC)–Korgas (PRC)–Altynkol (KAZ)–Almaty (KAZ)–Shu (KAZ)–Shymkent (KAZ)–Saksaulskaya (KAZ)–Aktobe (KAZ)–Kos Aral (RUS)**

    DRC 102 has a total length of about 3,500 km, with 31% electrified and 54% double-tracked. One of the more important features of DRC 102 is its long double-tracked distance. Also, there are no missing links in DRC 102. This is a corridor that utilizes the Korgas–Altynkol BCP, which opened in 2012. As indicated by the fact that the Chongqing (PRC)–Duisburg (Germany) container block train is running on this corridor, DRC 102 is recognized as an international freight rail corridor of high importance presently and in the future. The increase in utilization rate of this corridor is expected given the current low capacity usage of Korgas–Altynkol BCP so far (2 million tons/year for both directions). The main segment of DRC 102 overlaps with a route in the TAR.

---

[1] AFG = Afghanistan, AZE = Azerbaijan, PRC = People's Republic of China, GEO = Georgia, IRN = Islamic Republic of Iran, KAZ = Kazakstan, KGZ = Kyrgyz Republic, MON = Mongolia, PAK = Pakistan, RUS = Russian Federation, TAJ = Tajikistan, TKM = Turkmenistan, TUR = Turkey, and UZB = Uzbekistan.

Designated Rail Corridors 29

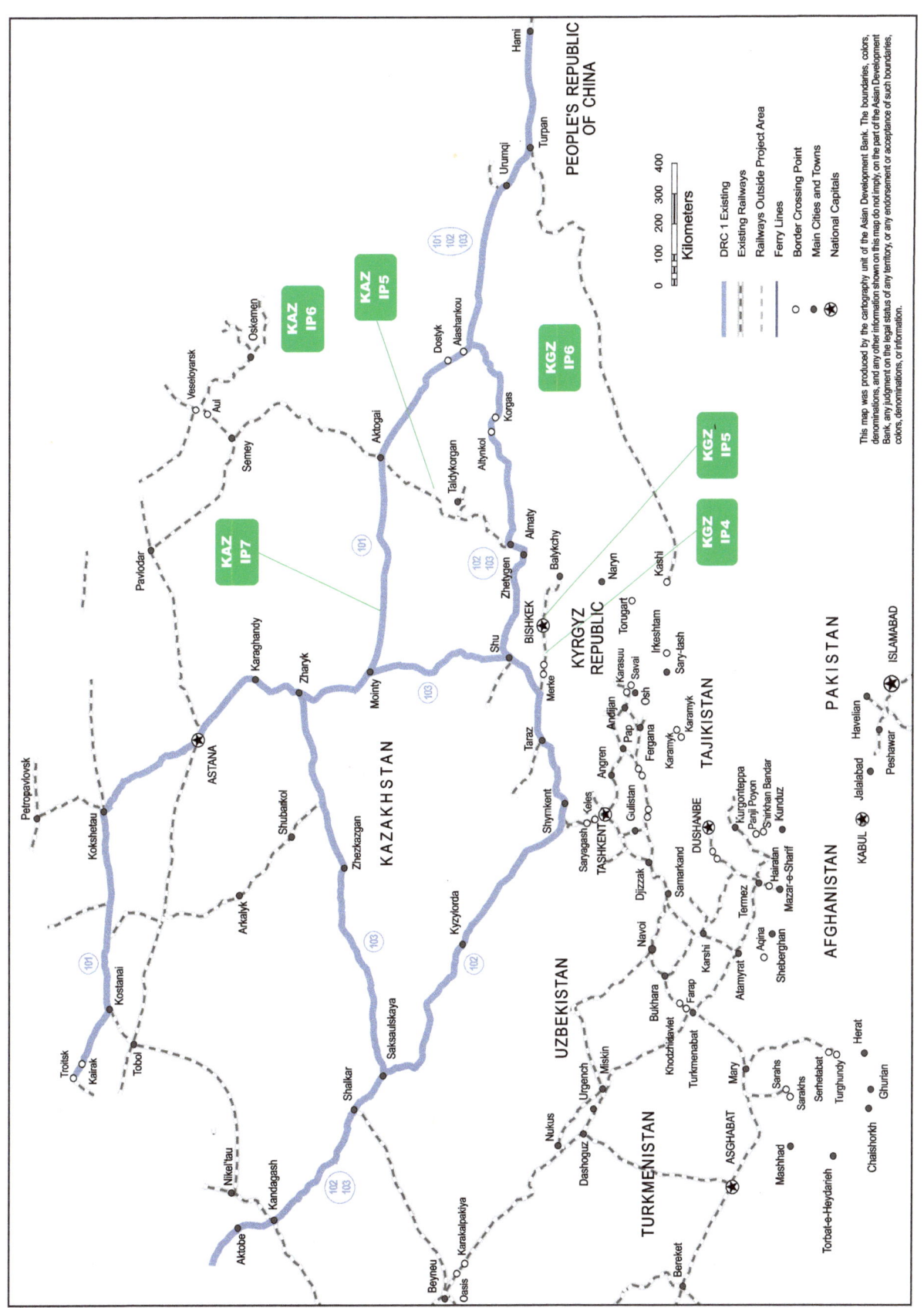

Map A3.1: Central Asia Regional Economic Cooperation Designated Rail Corridor 1: Europe–East Asia

Source: CAREC Secretariat.

- **DRC 103: Hami (PRC)–Urumqi (PRC)–Korgas (PRC)–Altynkol (KAZ)– Almaty (KAZ)–Shu (KAZ)–Mointy (KAZ)–Zharyk (KAZ)–Saksaulskaya (KAZ)–Aktobe (KAZ)–Kos Aral (RUS)**

  DRC 103 has a total length of about 3,700 km, with 32% electrified and 27% double-tracked. This corridor includes the Zhezkhazgan–Saksaulskaya section (KAZ IP13) completed in 2014, which likewise completes DRC 103. Currently DRC 103, especially for the Zhezkhazgan–Saksaulskaya section, seems to have low utilization rates of freight transport. However, DRC 103 is expected to increase its share of freight traffic volume in the future as it is expected to emerge as an important corridor connecting the PRC and Europe through the BCP of Korgas–Altynkol.

DRC 2: Mediterranean–East Asia

DRC 2 connects the PRC and Turkey/Southern Europe via Central Asia. Although, currently DRC 2 is not heavily used for rail freight traffic, this east-west connection will increase its importance depending on the economic growth of inland PRC and Turkey/Southern Europe. Issues concerning DRC 2 are its multimodal features (rail-port connection at Caspian Sea), the number of BCPs (passing through many borders), and the missing links which will require heavy investments of new rail construction. Four sub-corridors have been identified under DRC 2:

- **DRC 201: Hami (PRC)–Urumqi (PRC)–Alashankou (PRC)–Dostyk (KAZ)– Mointy (KAZ)–Zharyk (KAZ)–Saksaulskaya (KAZ)–Shalkar (KAZ)–Beyneu (KAZ)–Aktau (KAZ)–(Caspian Sea)–Alyat (AZE)–Baku (AZE)–Beyuk Kesik (AZE)–Gardabani (GEO)–Tbilisi (GEO)–Kars (TUR)**

  DRC 201 connects the PRC and Caucasus through Kazakhstan and the Caspian Sea. DRC 201 has a total length of about 4,200 km, with 24% electrified and 19% double-tracked. The recently completed section of Zhezkhazgan–Saksaulskaya (KAZ IP13) contributed to the completion of the DRC 201 route. About 800 km of electrification projects are planned in DRC 201 (KAZ IP6 and IP7). DRC 201 serves as the main route of the Mediterranean-East Asia connection as the rail network has been fully completed, while the rail-maritime connection in the Caspian Sea remains a major issue. The corridor will also extend to Georgia and Turkey with the completion of the Baku-Tbilisi-Kars Railway (BTK). The main portion of the DRC 201 overlaps with TRACECA's Trans-Caucasus route.

- **DRC 202: Hami (PRC)–Kashi (PRC)–Torugart (KGZ)–Savai (KGZ)– Karasuu (UZB)–Andijan (UZB)–Pap (UZB)–Tashkent (UZB)–Djizzak (UZB)–Samarkand (UZB)–Navoi (UZB)–Karakalpakiya (UZB)–Oasis (KAZ)–Beyneu (KAZ)– Aktau (KAZ)-(Caspian Sea)–Alyat (AZE)–Baku (AZE)–Beyuk Kesik (AZE)–Gardabani (GEO)–Tbilisi (GEO)–Kars (TUR)**

  DRC 202 connects the PRC, the Kyrgyz Republic, Uzbekistan, Kazakhstan and Azerbaijan. It includes a port connection to the Caspian Sea between the ports of Aktau (KAZ) and Aylat/Baku (AZE). The total length of DRC 202 is about 4,600 km, with 17% electrified and 17% double-tracked. A missing link of approximately (depending on final alignment) 500 km of railway in the Kyrgyz Republic including the

Designated Rail Corridors 31

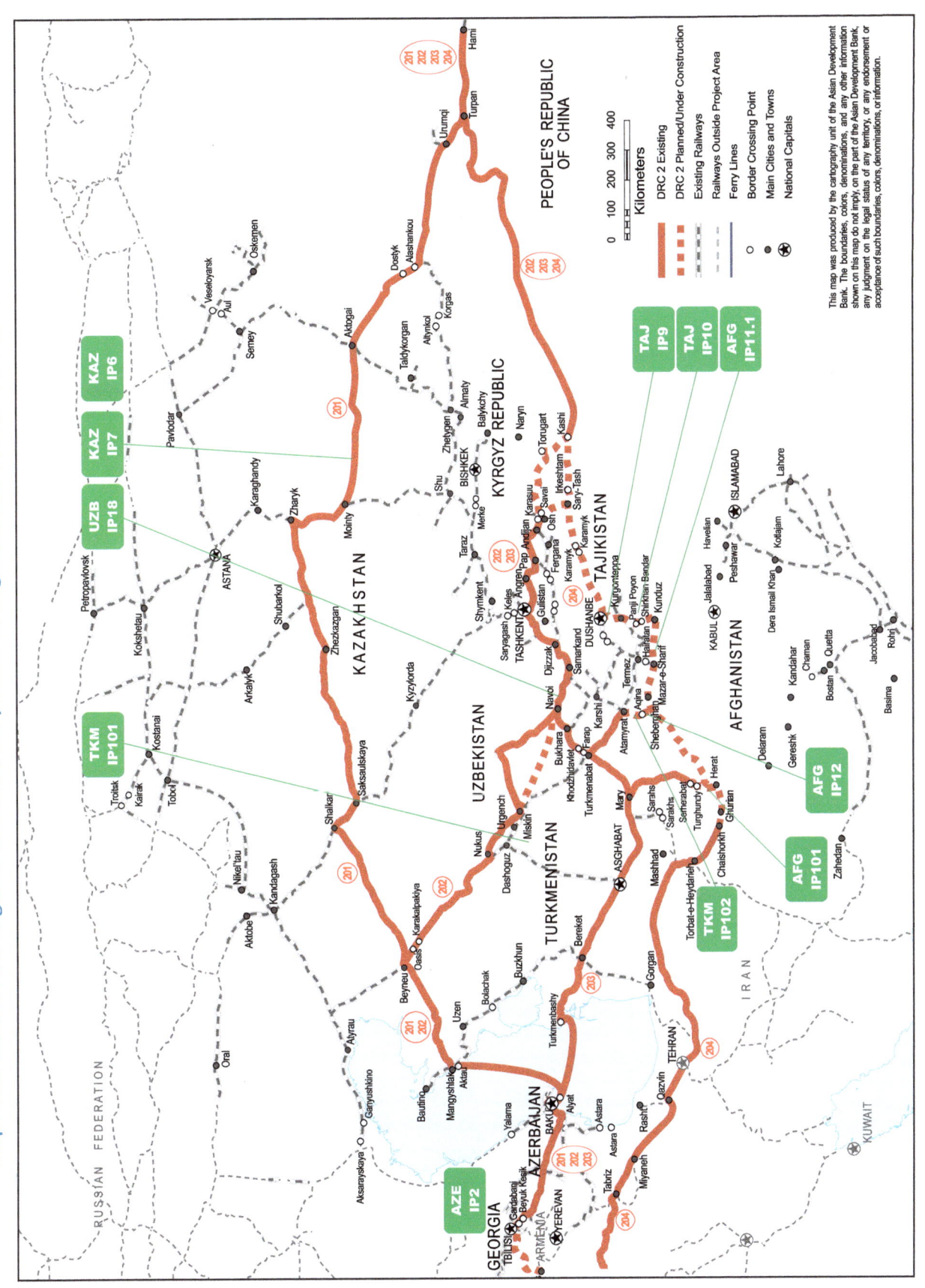

Map A3.2: Central Asia Regional Economic Cooperation Designated Rail Corridor 2: Mediterranean–East Asia

Source: CAREC Secretariat.

border crossing at Torugart (PRC and KGZ) is planned for construction. The factors that will impact the economic feasibility of this line include future transportation requirements, which in turn will also depend on the extent of industrialization of Xinjiang Uygur Autonomous Region of the PRC.

- **DRC 203: Hami (PRC)–Kashi (PRC)–Torugart (KGZ)–Savai (KGZ)–Karasuu (UZB)–Andijan (UZB)–Pap (UZB)–Tashkent (UZB)–Djizzak (UZB)–Samarkand (UZB)–Navoi (UZB)–Bukhara (UZB)–Khodzhidavlet (UZB)–Farap (TKM)–Turkmenabat (TKM)–Mary (TKM)–Ashghabat (TKM)–Turkmenbashi (TKM)– (Caspian Sea)–Alyat (AZE)–Baku (AZE)–Beyuk Kesik (AZE)–Gardabani (GEO)–Tbilisi (GEO)–Kars (TUR)**

DRC 203 is a similar route to DRC 202 except for the port connection at the Caspian Sea, where alternatively, DRC 203 uses the port of Turkmenbashi in Turkmenistan. The total length of DRC 203 is 4,300 km, with 19% electrified and 19% double tracked. A missing link, approximately 500 km of railway section in the Kyrgyz Republic including the border crossing at Torugart (PRC/KGZ) is new construction. The issue related to the construction in the Kyrgyz Republic is the same as DRC 202.

- **DRC 204: Hami (PRC)–Kashi (PRC)–Irkeshtam (KGZ)–Sary-tash (KGZ)–Karamyk (TAJ)–Dushanbe (TAJ)–Kurgonteppa (TAJ)–Panji Poyon (TAJ)–Shirkhan Bandar (AFG)–Kunduz (AFG)–Kholm (AFG)–Naibabad (AFG)–Mazar-e-Sharif (AFG)–Sheberghan (AFG)–Maimana (AFG)–Qalai Naw (AFG)–Kushk (AFG)–Herat (AFG)–Ghurian (AFG)–Chaishorkh (AFG)–Torbet-e-Heydarieh (IRN)–Teheran (IRN)–Tabriz (IRN)[2]**

DRC 204 is the rail corridor connecting the PRC, the Kyrgyz Republic, Tajikistan, Afghanistan and Iran. Out of the total length of 4,900 km, 1,700 km needs to be constructed. The construction sections include (i) Kashi–Irkeshtam in the PRC; (ii) Irkeshtam–Karamyk in Kyrgyz Republic; (iii) Vahdat–Karamyk and (iv) Kolkhozabad–Panji Poyon in Tajikistan; (v) Shirkhan Bandar–Mazar-e-Sharif–Sheberghan and (vi) Sheberghan–Herat in Afghanistan. Considering geographic conditions and the number of countries to cross, the rail construction for this corridor is quite ambitious, and thus economic and financial analyses are required to justify the construction. Economic Cooperation Organization (ECO) has been proposing this route.

DRC 3: Russian Federation–Middle East and South Asia

DRC 3 connects the Russian Federation and Iran via Central Asia. Although not characterized by high traffic volume, international rail freight is transported along this route. Given the strategic importance of the port of Bandar Abbas and the potential economic growth in Iran, the future expansion of the use of DRC 3 is expected.

---

[2] The following two extensions connecting DRC 203 and 204 are also included in DRC 204. These are: (i) Sheberghan (AFG)–Aqina (AFG)–Atamyrat (TKM)–Turkmenabat (TKM) and (ii) Herat (AFG)–Torghundi (AFG)–Serhetabat (TKM)–Mary (TKM).

- **DRC 301:** Veseloyarsk (RUS)–Aul (KAZ)–Aktogai (KAZ)–Almaty (KAZ)–Shymkent (KAZ)–Saryagash (KAZ)–Keles (UZB)–Tashkent (UZB)–Samarkand (UZB)–Navoi (UZB)–Khodzhidavlet (UZB)–Farap (TKM)–Turkmenabat (TKM)–Mary (TKM)–Serahs (TKM)–Sarakhs (IRN)–Bandar Abbas (IRN)

DRC 301 is a main rail route of connecting the Russian Federation, Kazakhstan, Uzbekistan, Turkmenistan and Iran. DRC 301 has a total distance of 4,100 km, with 29% electrified and 44% double-tracked. There are no missing links along this route. Currently, a significant amount of international traffic is expected to move along DRC 301, specifically at the Russian Federation–Kazakhstan border (Veseloyarsk/Aul), 7.5 million tons/year into Kazakhstan, while 2.3 million tons/year cross the Turkmenistan–Iran border (Serahs/Sarakhs). A future increase in rail freight in DRC 301 is expected given the strategic importance of Bandar Abbas port in Iran. A major section of DRC 301 overlaps with one of the ECO corridors, where ECO did trial-runs of trains through the corridor.

- **DRC302:** Veseloyarsk (RUS)–Aul (KAZ)–Aktogai (KAZ)–Almaty (KAZ)–Shymkent (KAZ)–Saryagash(KAZ)–Keles (UZB)–Tashkent (UZB)–Samarkand (UZB)–Karshi (UZB)–Termez (UZB)–Hairatan (AFG)–Mazar-e-Sharif (AFG)–Sheberghan (AFG)–Herat (AFG)–Ghurian (AFG)–Chaishorkh (AFG)

DRC 302 connects the Russian Federation, Kazakhstan, Uzbekistan, Afghanistan and Iran. Out of the total length of 3,400 km, about 550 km of the Afghanistan section is yet to be constructed. This route is 38% electrified and double tracked. Improvement of security and economic growth of Afghanistan are keys to the future usage of DRC 302 and justification of the construction of the missing link.

DRC 4: Russian Federation–East Asia

DRC 4 is the route through Mongolia that connects the Russian Federation and the PRC. The corridor is the Trans-Mongolian section of the Trans-Siberian Railway. The direction of movement for bulk of the traffic is toward the PRC. There is about 1.5–2.0 million tonnes of transit traffic moving to the PRC through this corridor. The bulk of the transit traffic currently from the PRC utilizes the Trans-Siberian Route.

- **DRC 401:** Naushki (RUS)–Sukhbaatar (MON)–Zamiin-Uud (MON)–Erenhot (PRC)

The main track is 900 km long, with the entire length single-tracked and non-electrified. Capacity expansion for this rail corridor is planned by the operator.

Map A3.3: Central Asia Regional Economic Cooperation Designated Rail Corridor 3: Russian Federation–Middle East and South Asia

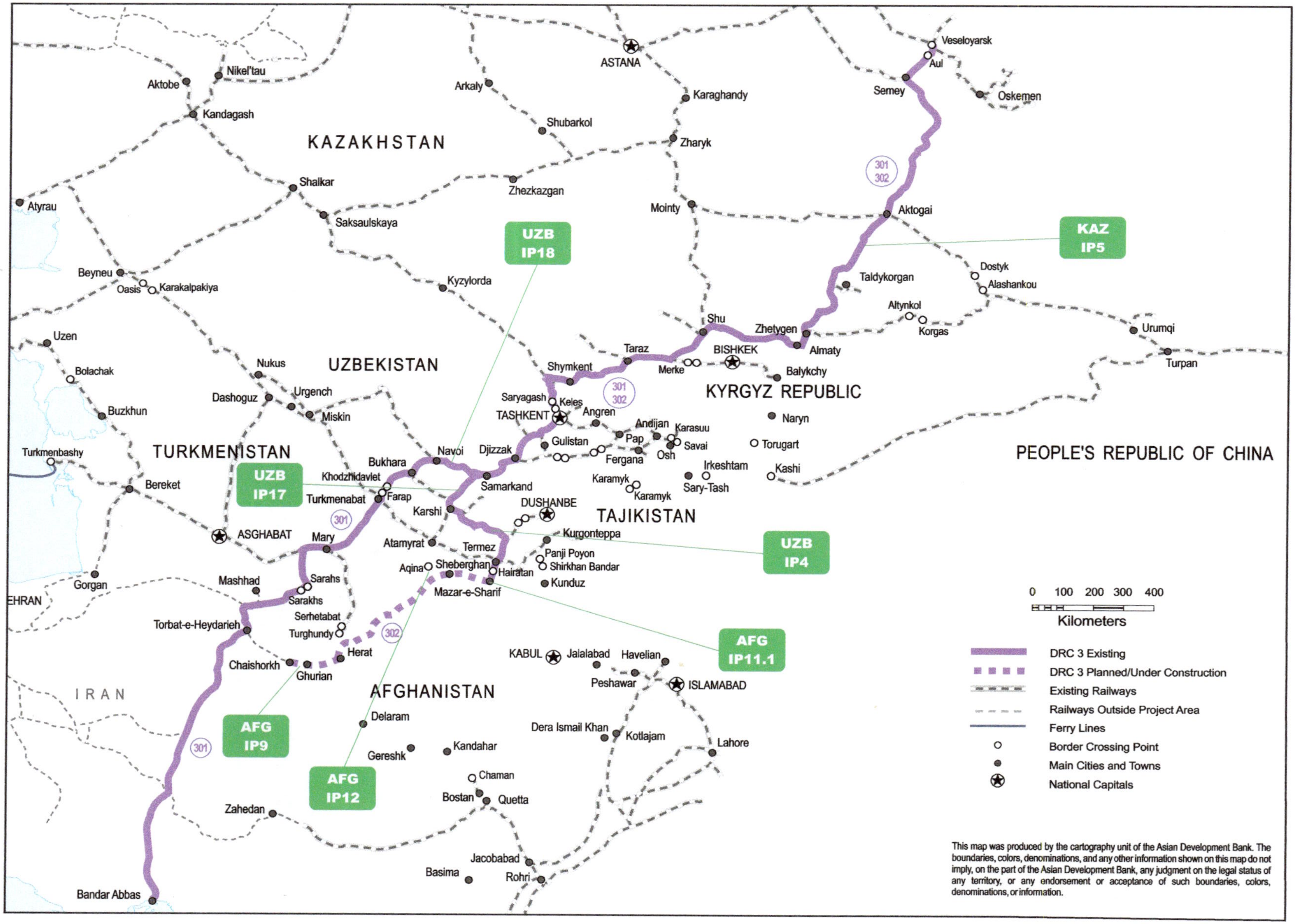

Source: CAREC Secretariat.

Designated Rail Corridors 35

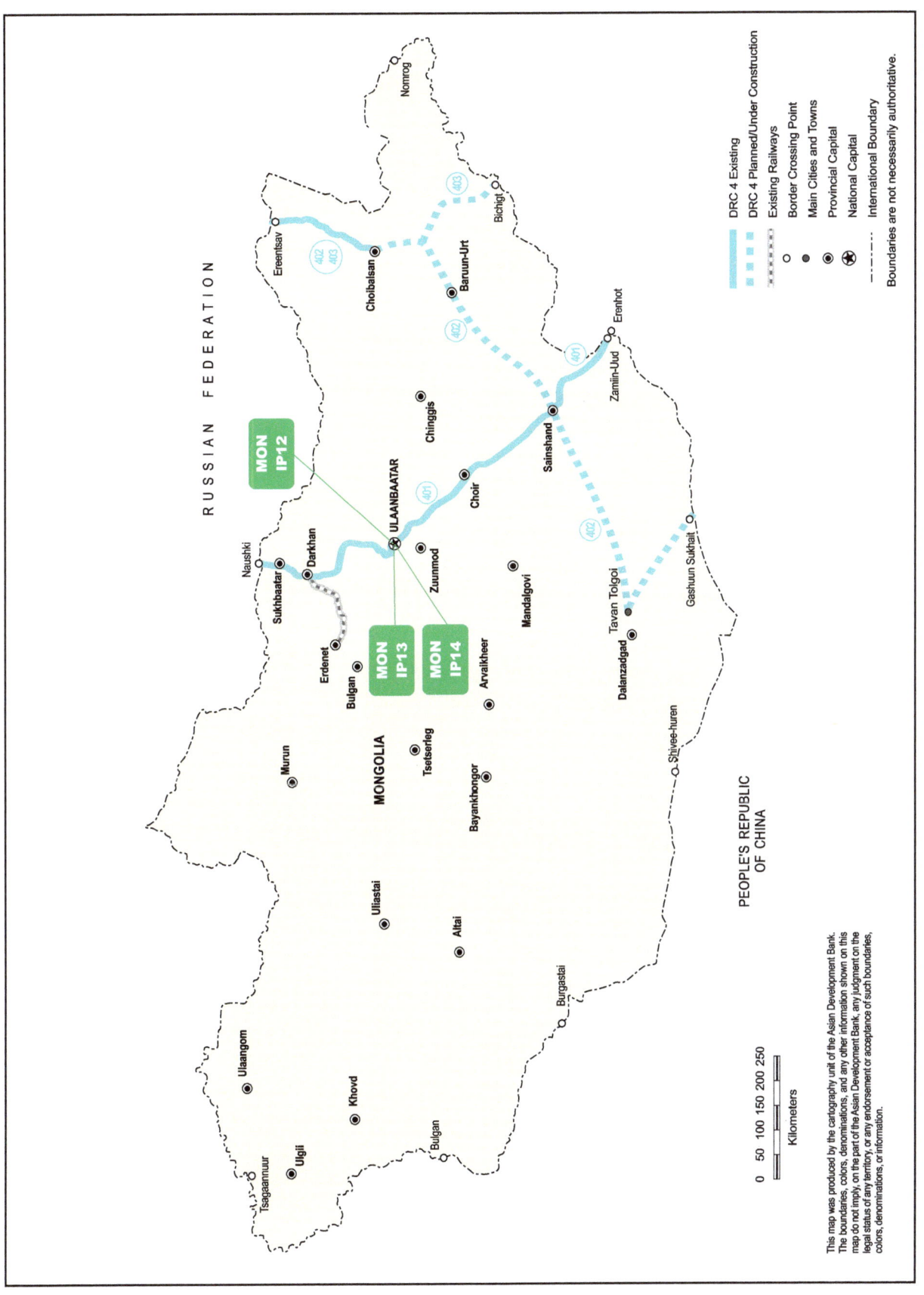

Map A3.4: Central Asia Regional Economic Cooperation Designated Rail Corridor 4: Russian Federation–East Asia

Source: CAREC Secretariat.

- **DRC 402: Ereentsav (Mongolia's border with the Russian Federation)–Baruun-urt (MON)–Sainshand (MON)–Tavan Tolgoi–Gashuun Sukhait (Mongolia's border with the PRC)**

  The main purpose of this line would be for transporting coal from Tavan Tolgoi mines to the PRC or eastward. Construction of a new railway line from Sainshand to Tavan Tolgoi, from Tavan Tolgoi to Gashuun Sukhait, and Sainshand to Choibalsan would be required. The total length of this line is about 1,400 km. The railway section that is existing but would require rehabilitation is the section from Choibalsan to the border with the Russian Federation. Some construction work on the Tavan Tolgoi–Gashuun Sukhait section has already started.

- **DRC 403: Ereentsav (Mongolia's border with the Russian Federation)–Choibalsan (MON)–Bichigt (Mongolia's border with the PRC)**

  This corridor connects the border with the Russian Federation at Selovyevsk to the border with the PRC at Zuun Khatavch. Construction would be required from Choibalsan to Bichigt. The railway line from Choibalsan to the border with the Russian Federation already exists and would only require rehabilitation.

DRC 5: East Asia–Middle East and South Asia

DRC 5 is the rail corridor connecting the PRC and Pakistan. DRC 5 is aiming to link the PRC and the ports along the coast of the Arabian Sea, such as Karachi and Gwadar ports. The rail freight market demand will depend on the future industrialization expansion of inner PRC regions, and on mineral resource development in Afghanistan. DRC 5 includes major missing links at the borders of the PRC and Pakistan and at the long sections traversing Afghanistan. For both missing links, the economic and financial feasibility should be reviewed to justify construction.

- **DRC 501: Hami (PRC)–Kashi (PRC)–Islamabad (PAK)–Lahore (PAK)–Karachi (PAK)**

  DRC 501 will connect Hami, PRC to Karachi, Pakistan. Out of the total length of 3,800 km, about 700 km of railways crossing the border of the PRC and Pakistan remains to be constructed. The section of the railway located in Pakistan is mainly double-tracked, roughly comprising 32% of the total length. As the border area of the PRC and Pakistan is located in the Karakoram mountain range, the construction of this railway is highly ambitious in terms of cost and technical difficulty. In Pakistan, the Islamabad–Lahore–Karachi section consists of the ML-1, which is one of the most important rail corridors in Pakistan. ML-1 caters to more than 70% of Pakistan's existing rail operations, and thus, it is being upgraded to enhance its capacity.

- **DRC 502: Hami (PRC)–Kashi (PRC)–Quetta (PAK)–Gwadar (PAK)**

  DRC 502 will connect the PRC and Pakistan, from Hami to the port of Gwadar. Out of the total length of 3,600 km, about 2,100 km is yet to be constructed. Construction of railway at the borders of the PRC and Pakistan is highly ambitious, as similarly mentioned for DRC 501. Also, almost all railway sections

Designated Rail Corridors 37

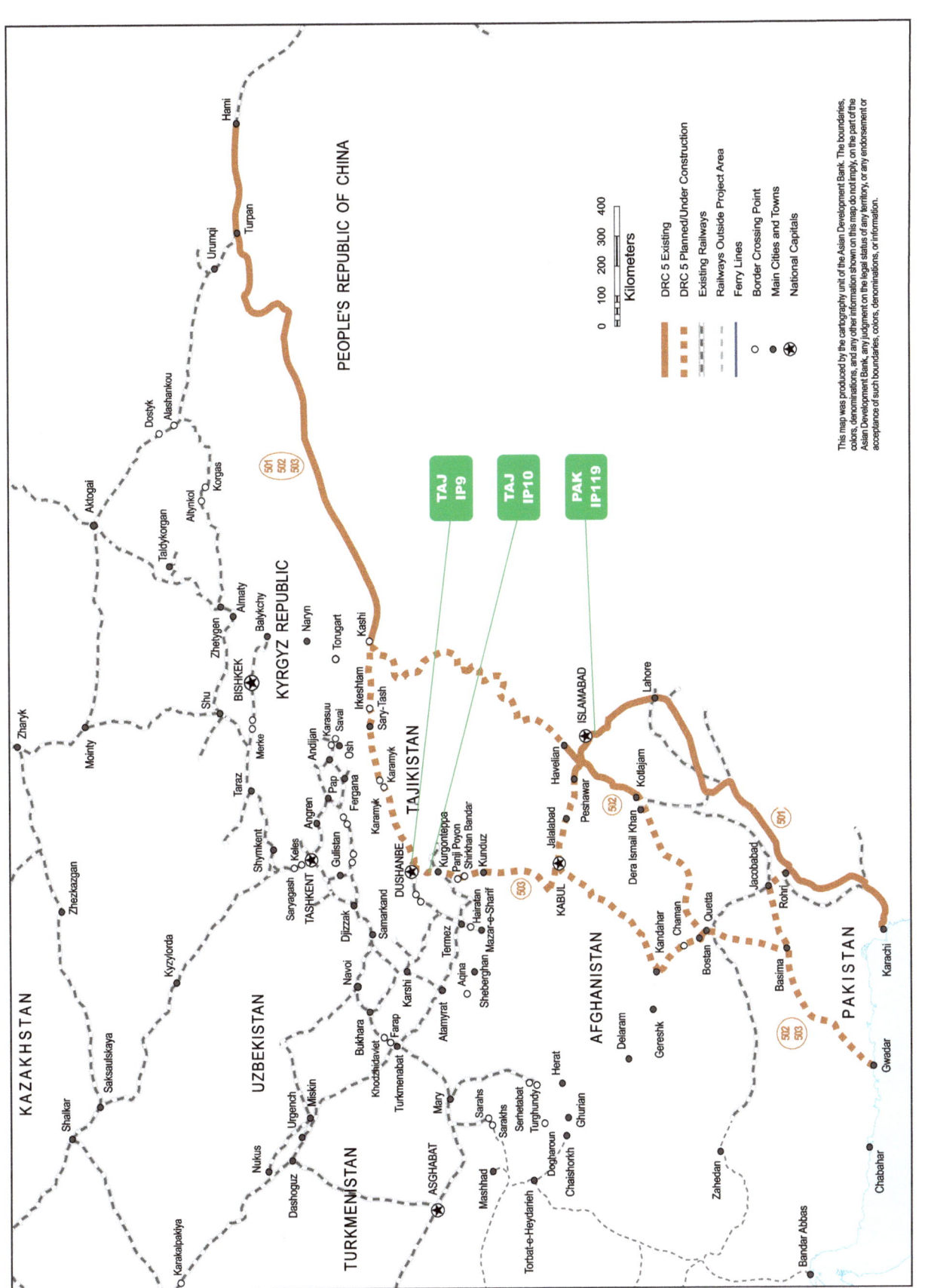

Map A3.5: Central Asia Regional Economic Cooperation Designated Rail Corridor 5: East Asia–Middle East and South Asia

Source: CAREC Secretariat.

in Pakistan are new construction. Economic and financial feasibilities are essential in the justification of DRC 502 as a rail corridor project.

- **DRC 503: Hami (PRC)–Kashi (PRC)–Irkeshtam (KGZ)–Sary-tash (KGZ)–Karamyk (TAJ)–Dushanbe (TAJ)–Kurgonteppa (TAJ)–Panji Poyon (TAJ)–Shirkhan Bandar (AFG)–Kunduz (AFG)–Kabul (AFG)–Kandahar (AFG)–Chaman (PAK)–Quetta (PAK)–Gwadar (PAK)[3]**

    DRC 503 will connect the PRC, the Kyrgyz Republic, Tajikistan, Afghanistan, and Pakistan by rail. Out of 4,100 km total length, more than half is yet to be constructed. The development of this DRC is dependent on the market requirements along this route, and the impact of its connection to the port of Gwadar. In Pakistan, a feasibility study for a new railway line that links Gwadar with Quetta and Jacobabad via Basima has been initiated.

DRC 6: Europe–Middle East and South Asia

DRC 6 is the rail corridor that connects Europe to Iran and Pakistan, which is aiming to link the hinterland cities to the ports of the Persian Gulf and Arabian Sea (e.g. Bandar Abbas port in Iran and Karachi/Gwadar port in Pakistan). This corridor will form a port-hinterland connection in line with the expansion of the market needs of the related regions.

- **DRC 601: Poti/Batumi (GEO)–Gardabani (GEO)–Beyuk Kesik (AZE)–Astara (AZE and IRN)–Teheran (IRN)–Bandar Abbas (IRN)**

    This corridor includes the 503 km east-west main line in Azerbaijan and the railway line in Georgia from Poti/Batumi (GEO) to Beyuk Kesik. The Baku-Tbilisi-Kars (BTK) line to Turkey is also part of this corridor. Currently, the total DRC length has 32% double track and 12% electrified lengths. All of these lines (including the BTK when completed in 2017) will be upgraded to double track and electrified. The route follows Azerbaijan's east-west main line and connects with its north–south line near Baku. Construction of an 8 km missing link between Azerbaijan and Iran at the southernmost section of the north–south line and completion of the on-going construction of a 170 km railway line from Rasht to Astara in Iran will connect the corridor to Bandar Abbas port in Iran.

- **DRC 602: Yalama (AZE)–Baku (AZE)–Astara (AZE and IRN)–Teheran (IRN)–Bandar Abbas (IRN)**

    The North–South Transport Corridor is part of an ancient trading route that has connected South Asia with Northern Europe for centuries. There are two railway corridors on each side of the Caspian Sea. The corridor located west of the Caspian Sea is comprised of a southern segment with length of 438 km. This is a railway line that extends from Yalama (the border between Azerbaijan and

---

[3] The following extension is also included in DRC 503: Kabul (AFG)–Jalalabad (AFG)–Peshawar (PAK)–D.I. Khan (PAK)–Zhoab (PAK)–Quetta (PAK)–Gwadar (PAK).

Designated Rail Corridors 39

Map A3.6: Central Asia Regional Economic Cooperation Designated Rail Corridor 6: Europe–Middle East and South Asia

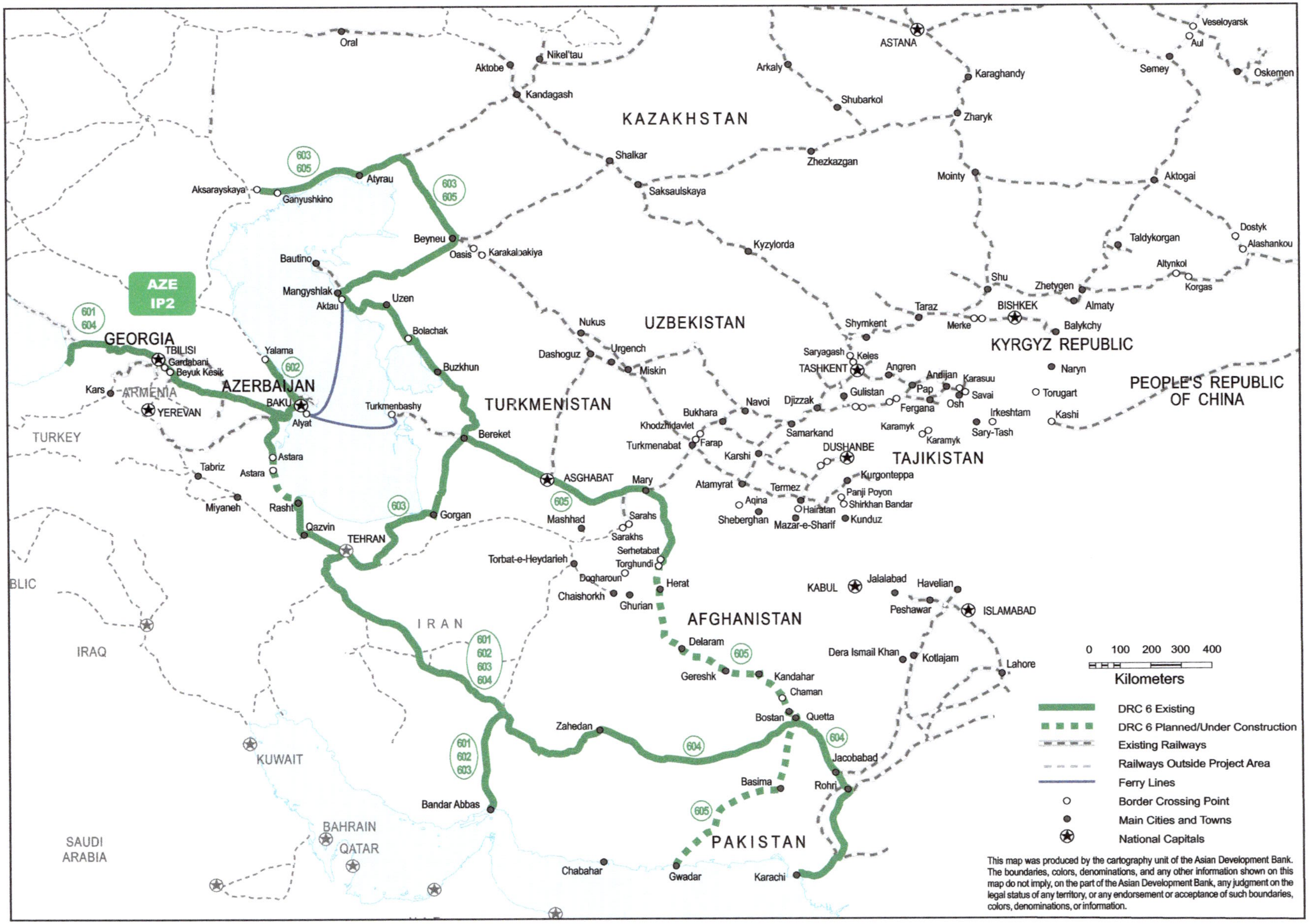

Source: CAREC Secretariat.

the Russian Federation) to Astara, which is about 8 km from Azerbaijan's border with Iran. The northern section of this line (from Yalama to Alyat) is double tracked and electrified. However, most sections of this line require track rehabilitation. Iran is constructing a 170 km line from Rasht to its border with Azerbaijan. If an 8 km section linking Azerbaijan and Iran were built, the route would connect the Russian Federation through Iran and to Bandar Abbas. The estimated total length of this corridor is 2,100 km.

- **DRC 603: Aksarayskaya (RUS)–Ganyushkino (KAZ)–Beyneu (KAZ)–Uzen (KAZ)–Bolachak (KAZ)–Bereket (TKM)–Gorgan (IRN)–Teheran (IRN)–Bandar Abbas (IRN)**

This North–South Transport Corridor, located on the eastern side of the Caspian Sea, connects Kazakhstan, Turkmenistan and Iran. The total length is about 3,600 km. DRC 603 only has 100 km of electrified line (Tehran–Garmsar) and a relatively larger proportion of double track lines at 17%. Along this route, the Turkmenistan section has been developed recently under Islamic Development Bank financing. Also on-going is its signalization to enhance the traffic capacity under ADB financing (the North–South Railway Project). There are no missing links in DRC 603. DRC 603 will be an important international rail corridor not only for enhancing port access from Kazakhstan and Turkmenistan, but also as a major transport link between Europe and the Middle East.

- **DRC 604 Poti/Batumi (GEO)–Gardabani (GEO)–Beyuk Kesik (AZE)–Astara (AZE and IRN)–Teheran (IRN)–Zahedan (IRN)–Quetta (PAK)–Karachi (PAK)[4]**

This corridor requires construction of an eight-km link between Azerbaijan and Iran. Also, in Pakistan, upgradation of ML-3 (Jacobabad–Quetta–Taftan) and extension of ML-2 (a new rail line from Gwadar to Quetta and Jacobabad via Basima) will improve connectivity to Karachi port and link Gwardar port. The route is envisioned to be the shortest land-based route between Karachi and Northern Europe.

- **DRC605 Aksarayskaya (RUS)–Ganyushkino (KAZ)–Beyneu (KAZ)–Uzen (KAZ)–Bolachak (KAZ)–Bereket (TKM)–Ashgabat (TKM)–Mary (TKM)–Serhetabat (TKM)–Torghundi (AFG)–Herat (AFG)–Kandahar (AFG)–Chaman (PAK)–Quetta (PAK)–Karachi (PAK)[5]**

This corridor connects the Russian Federation and the ports of Pakistan (Karachi and Gwadar) through Turkmenistan, Afghanistan and Pakistan. This route requires the development of railway sections in Afghanistan. Also, in Pakistan, the new construction between Quetta and Gwadar is needed. This is a 4,100-km line with 80% of the line already in operation.

A summary of technical features of each corridor is indicated in Table A3.1.

---

[4] The extension of Quetta (PAK)–Gwadar (PAK) is included in DRC604.
[5] The extension of Quetta (PAK)–Gwadar (PAK) is included in DRC605.

Table A3.1: CAREC Designated Rail Corridors: Summary of Technical Features

Corridor	DRC	Total Length km	Existing Length km	Existing Length %	Electrified Length km	Electrified Length %	Double Tracked Length km	Double Tracked Length %
1	101	3,100	3,100	100	1,100	35	900	29
	102	3,500	3,500	100	1,100	31	1,900	54
	103	3,700	3,700	100	1,200	32	1,000	27
Corridor 1 Subtotal		7,000	7,000	100	2,300	33	3,000	43
2	201	4,200	4,200	100	1,000	24	800	19
	202	4,600	4,200	91	800	17	800	17
	203	4,300	3,900	91	800	19	800	19
	204	4,900	3,200	65	–	0	900	18
Corridor 2 Subtotal		12,300	10,000	81	1,400	11	2,000	16
3	301	4,100	4,100	100	1,200	29	1,800	44
	302	3,400	2,800	82	1,300	38	1,300	38
Corridor 3 Subtotal		5,400	4,800	89	1,300	24	1,800	23
4	401	900	900	100	–	0	0	0
	402	1,400	200	14	–	0	0	0
	403	500	200	40	–	0	0	0
Corridor 4 Subtotal		2,500	1,100	44	–	0	0	0
5	501	3,800	3,100	82	300	8	1,200	32
	502	3,600	1,500	42	–	0	0	0
	503	4,100	1,500	37	–	0	0	0
Corridor 5 Subtotal		7,000	3,100	44	300	4	1,200	17
6	601	2,500	2,300	92	300	12	800	32
	602	2,100	1,900	90	300	14	800	38
	603	3,600	3,600	100	100	3	600	17
	604	4,000	3,900	98	300	8	900	23
	605	4,100	3,300	80	–	0	400	10
Corridor 6 Subtotal		9,600	8,600	90	800	8	2,000	17
Total		**32,400**	**25,200**	**78**	**3,900**	**12**	**7,000**	**22**

CAREC = Central Asia Regional Economic Cooperation, DRC = Designated Rail Corridor, km = kilometer.
Note: The total does not match the aggregation of each corridor due to the overlapping sections.
Source: CAREC Secretariat.

APPENDIX 4
Priority Investment Projects

CAREC TTFS2020 has indicated a priority investment project (IP) list for railways, which has been updated year-by-year. In addition to this original list, new potential railway projects which were proposed by each country's presentation at the first railway working group in November 2015, have been temporarily added to the IP list (next page). The implementation period of investment has been divided into 2017–2020 and 2021–2030. The total project cost is estimated as $38 billion ($8 billion for IP and $30 billion for potential projects), and the total length to be developed/modernized will be approximately 18,000 kilometers (km) (5,000 km for IP and 13,000 km for potential projects). The distribution of investment by implementation period, country (2017–2020), and corridor (2017–2020) is shown in Figures A4.1, A4.2 and A4.3.

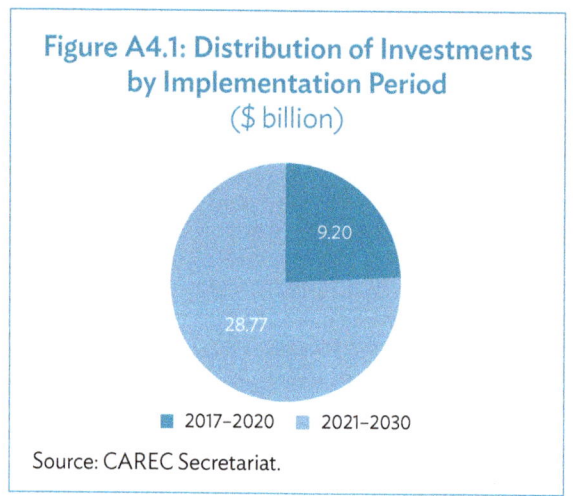

Figure A4.1: Distribution of Investments by Implementation Period ($ billion)

Source: CAREC Secretariat.

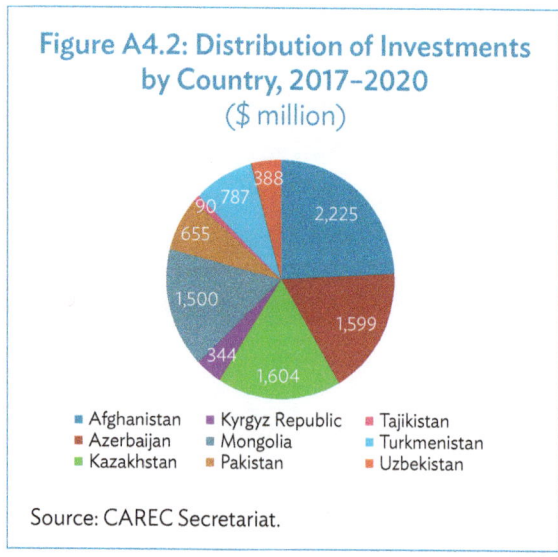

Figure A4.2: Distribution of Investments by Country, 2017–2020 ($ million)

Source: CAREC Secretariat.

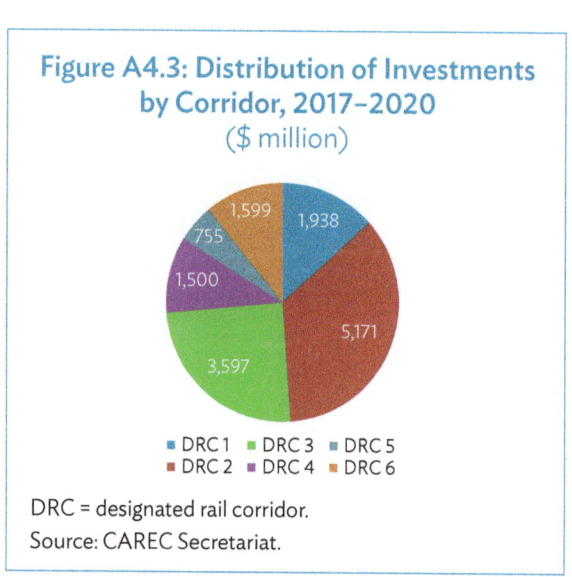

Figure A4.3: Distribution of Investments by Corridor, 2017–2020 ($ million)

DRC = designated rail corridor.
Source: CAREC Secretariat.

Table A4.1: List of Railway Investment Projects

Country	IP No.	Project Title	Priority Investment Projects Cost Estimate ($ million)	Km	Potential Projects Proposed by Country Cost Estimate ($ million)	Km	Status	Implementation Period
Afghanistan	IP 9	Rozanak/Ghorian–Herat Airport Railway Line Construction (Iran–Afghanistan)	150	87			FS completed	2017–2018
	IP 11.1	Construction of Shirkhan Bandar–Kunduz–Kholam–Naibabad/Mazar-e-Sherif–Sheberghan– Andkhoy–Meimana–Qala-e-Naw–Herat Railway	2,000	1,000			FS completed	2017–2020
	IP 12	Construction of Aqina–Andkhoy Railway (Turkmenistan–Afghanistan)	75	38			FS completed	2017–2020
	IP 101	Construction of Turghondy–Herat Airport Railway		170			FS in progress	2017–2020
		Kunduz–Baghlan–Bamyan–Parwan–Kabul Railway				400	FS completed	2020–2030
		Kabul–Torkham Railway				224	PFS completed	2020–2030
		Kabul–Ghazi–Kandahar Railway				500	PFS completed	2020–2030
		Kandahar–Helmand–Farah–Herat Railway				620	PFS completed	2020–2030
		Kandahar–Spin Boldak Railway				96	PFS completed	2020–2030
		Kunduz–Qala e Mafushad Railway				600	Concept	2020–2030
		Subtotal	2,225	1,295	0	2,440		
Azerbaijan	IP 2	Railway Trade and Transport Facilitation	1,599	317			East West Line Rehab on-going	2017–2020
				192			North South Rehabilitation–Gov't priority	2017–2020
		Subtotal	1,599	509	0	0		
Kazakhstan	IP 5	Electrification of Almaty–Aktogay Railway Section	984	541			Gov't priority	2017–2020
	IP 6	Electrification of Dostyk–Aktogay Railway Section	510	309			Gov't priority	2017–2020
	IP 7	Electrification of Aktogay–Mointy Railway Section	110	522			Gov't priority	2017–2020
		Subtotal	1,604	1,372	0	0		
Kyrgyz Republic	IP 4	Electrification of Lugovaya–Bishkek (Alamedin) Railway	250	157			Study needed	2017–2020
	IP 5	Rehabilitation of Balykchy–Chaldovar–Lugovaya Railroad	66	323			Gov't priority	2017–2020
	IP 6	Equipment Purchase for Wagon Repair/Maintenance Facility for Rail	18	0			Gov't priority	2017–2020

continued on next page

Table A4.1 continued

Country	IP No.	Project Title	Priority Investment Projects Cost Estimate ($ million)	Km	Potential Projects Proposed by Country Cost Estimate ($ million)	Km	Status	Implementation Period
Kyrgyz Republic		Balyychy–Kochkor–Kara-Keche Railway				190	FS in progress	2020–2030
		Alamedin Terminal Improvement			10	0	Gov't priority	2017–2020
		Torugart–Jalalabad Railway			5,000		Study needed. 2 Main Options: (i) North via At Bashy (472 km); (ii) South 276 km.	2020–2030
		Irkeshtam–Karamik Railway (PRC–KGZ–TAJ)					Study needed	2020–2030
		Subtotal	334	480	5,010	190		
Mongolia	IP 12	Railway Rolling Stock Maintenance Depot	59	0			Gov't priority	2020–2030
	IP 13	Railway Centralized Traffic Control Center	29	0			Gov't priority	2020–2030
	IP 14	Ulaanbaatar City Railway Passenger Station	36	0			Gov't priority	2020–2030
		Bogdkhan Railway Bypass Project			500		Gov't priority (ADB PPTA 2016)	2017–2020
		UBTZ Capacity Expansion (double tracking, electrification, signalling, operations, organization)			1,000	1,110	FS completed	2017–2020
		New Railway Lines Southern Mongolia			5,000	1,800	Gov't priority (PPP)	2020–2030
		Subtotal	124	0	6,500	2,910		
Pakistan	IP 119	Lahore–Peshawar Railway Rehabilitation	665	463			Gov't priority	2017–2020
		Lahore–Karachi Railway Upgrading (ML-1)				1218	Study needed	2020–2030
		Upgrading ML-2 Kotri-Attock				1427	Study needed	2020–2030
		Havelian Dry Port Construction				0	Study needed	2020–2030
		Jaccobad–Gwadar Railway			4,000	1,050	PFS completed	2020–2030
		Jaccobad–Quetta Railway (ML-3) Upgrading			150	295	PFS completed	2020–2030
		Quetta–Taftan Railway (ML-3) Upgrading			1,000	680	PFS completed	2020–2030
		Quetta–Kotlajam Railway Construction			1,500	560	PFS completed	2020–2030
		Chaman–Spin Boldak Railway Construction				12	Study needed	2020–2030
		Peshawar–Jalalabad Railway Construction				145	FS in progress	2020–2030

continued on next page

Table A4.1　continued

Country	IP No.	Project Title	Priority Investment Projects Cost Estimate ($ million)	Km	Potential Projects Proposed by Country Cost Estimate ($ million)	Km	Status	Implementation Period
Pakistan		Havelian–Khunjerab Railway Construction			12,000	682	Concept	2020–2030
		Subtotal	665	463	18,650	6,069		
Tajikistan	IP 10	Construction of railway Kolkhozabad–Dusti–Nizhnyi–Pyandj–Afghanistan Border	90	50			Ongoing	2017–2020
		Construction of Vakhdat–Karamik Railway				296		2020–2030
		Construction of North–South Railway				280		2020–2030
		Installation of fiber optic cable communication line along Dushanbe–Kurgan-Tyube railway section				129	PFS completed	2020–2030
		Subtotal	90	50	0	705		
Turkmenistan	IP 101	Construction of Dashoguz–Shasenem–Gazojak Railway	490	212			Gov't priority	2017–2020
	IP 102	Construction of Atamyrat–Ymamnazar–Aqina Railway	297	85			Ongoing	2017–2020
		Railway modernization						2017–2020
		Subtotal	787	297	0	0		
Uzbekistan	IP 4	Electrification of Karshi–Termez Railway Section	388	325			Ongoing	2017
		Pap–Namangan-Andijan Railway Electrification				145	Gov't priority	2017–2020
		Navoi-Kanimekh-Miskent Railway Construction				326	Gov't priority	2017
		Subtotal	388	325	0	471		
Total			7,816	4,791	30,160	12,785		

FS = Feasibility Study, IP = Priority Investment Project, km = kilometer, PFS = Pre Feasibility Study.
Source: CAREC Secretariat.

APPENDIX 5
Rail Infrastructure Project Prioritization Methodology

Introduction

Infrastructure project prioritization is about evaluating, comparing and ranking projects, in order to invest in those (and spend scarce funds) that generate maximum benefits to the economy and society as a whole.

The estimation of financial benefits of infrastructure projects is often relatively easy, while the effects of the infrastructure on e.g. the natural or cultural environment are highly difficult to express in monetary terms. Still, such nonmonetary impacts cannot be ignored.

In between these two types of benefits are various other impacts of infrastructure development, such as air pollution, traffic safety, noise, and travel times. For some there is a methodology in place to monetize these effects. Others have to be evaluated in a qualitative way.

Moreover, considering the scarcity of funds available and the need for infrastructure improvements, it is essential to follow a coherent investment planning that takes into account the feasibility and risks of implementation.

Cost–Benefit Analysis and Multi-Criteria Analysis: People, Planet, and Profit

Evaluating and prioritizing infrastructure projects (particularly the highly capital-intensive ones) is usually causing intensive discussions since it involves many stakeholders. Economists, companies, politicians, civilians, town and country planners, authorities, ecologists, bankers: all have something to contribute, and sometimes have conflicting views and interests. For this very reason it is of major importance to develop a transparent methodology to evaluate and prioritize projects.

The effects of an infrastructure project are numerous and can be grouped in various ways. One way to make a distinction refers to the classification People, Planet, and Profit (Figure A5.1). This structure—often referred to as the 3Ps—stems from the sustainable development theory, which says that all three components should be balanced to obtain sustainability. Since rail transport infrastructure has a major impact on all three categories, the 3Ps structure is suitable to classify the effects.

Applying the 3P structure to infrastructure project evaluation, it would look like Figure A5.2. Note that the matrix not only distinguishes impacts that relate to the 3Ps, but also indicates the degree to which these can be measured in monetary terms, or whether these are quantifiable at all.

Rail Infrastructure Project Prioritization Methodology

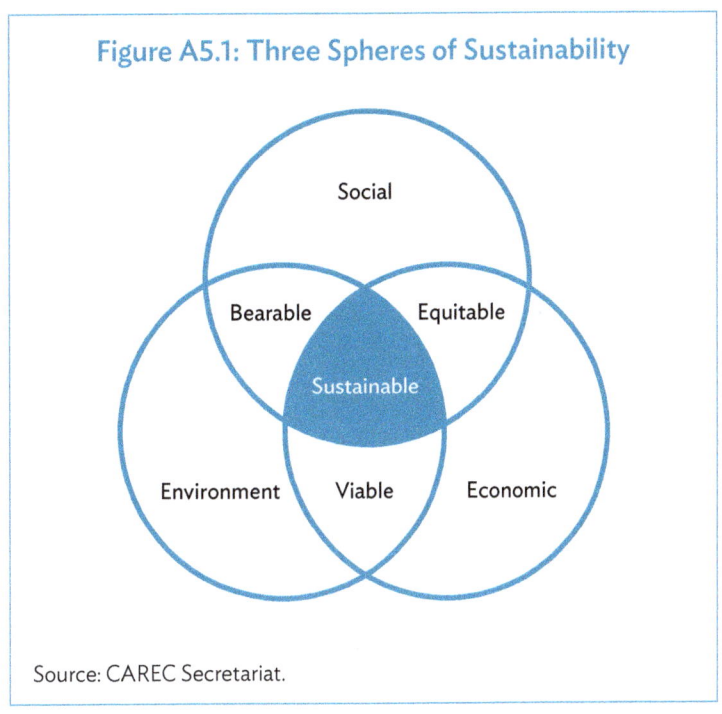

Figure A5.1: Three Spheres of Sustainability

Source: CAREC Secretariat.

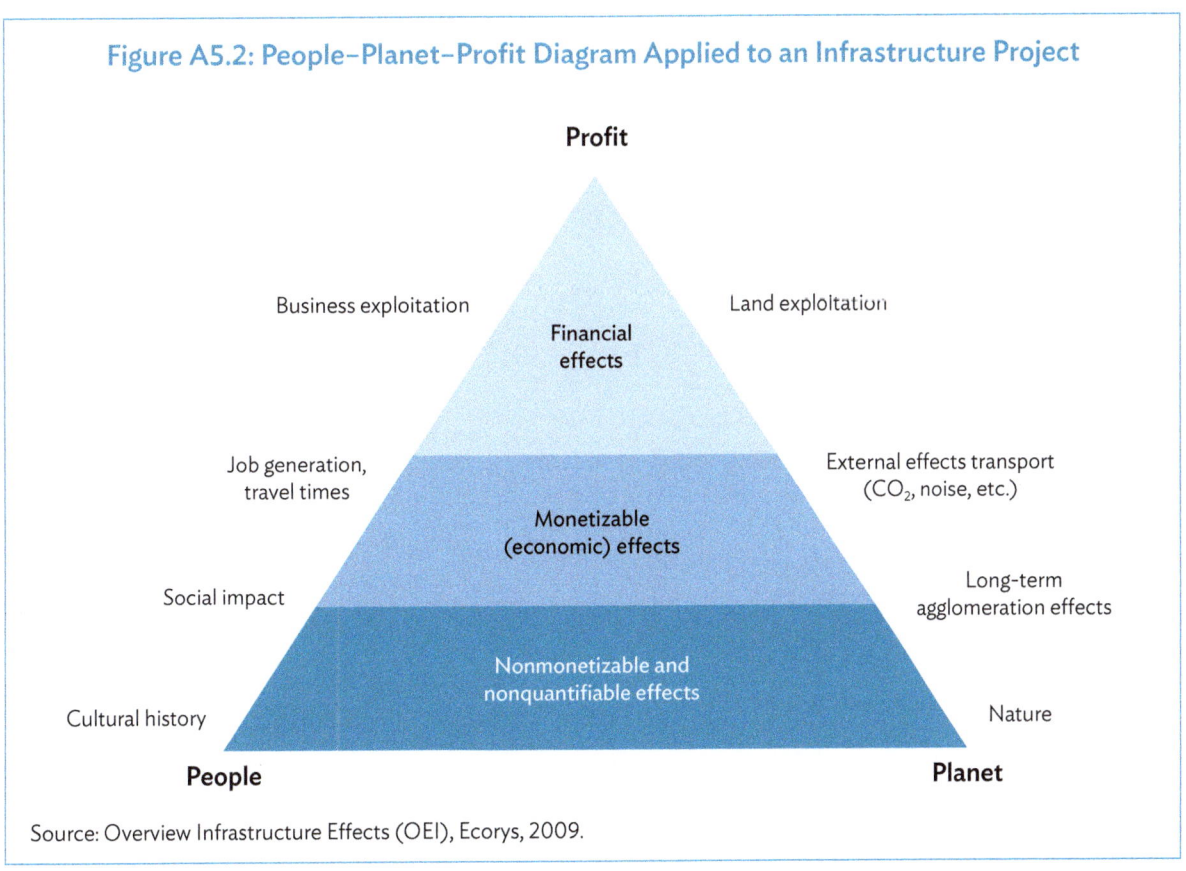

Figure A5.2: People–Planet–Profit Diagram Applied to an Infrastructure Project

Source: Overview Infrastructure Effects (OEI), Ecorys, 2009.

The financial cost–benefit analysis (CBA) provides an estimate of the financial rate of return (FIRR) and net present value that expresses the monetary impact on Profit. The economic rate of return (EIRR) and cost–benefit ratio expresses the quantified (in monetary terms) effects on Planet (e.g. air pollution) and People (social cost of accidents, employment). To include effects that cannot be expressed in monetary terms, or not quantified at all, a multi-criteria analysis (MCA) may be added to the quantitative analyses. An MCA can be structured along a matrix that indicates the type and strength of individual effects. Table A5.1 is an example of such an MCA matrix.

Table A5.1: Example Matrix of Nonmonetizable and/or Nonquantified Effects

	Objectives/Impacts	Projects		
		A	B	C
People	Strengthening of social infrastructure	1	2	1
People	Diversification of work- and living environment	2	2	2
Planet	Impact on nature and landscape	3	2	1
Planet	Impact on climate (e.g. shift from road to rail)	2	3	1
Profit	(Inter-)national competitiveness and attraction	2	2	1
Profit	Accessibility to (inter-)national infrastructure networks	3	2	1
Profit	Impact on the regional economy	2	2	3
Profit	Impact on the national economy	2	1	2
Feasibility and Risks	Technical risks	1	1	3
Feasibility and Risks	Investment required	1	1	3
Feasibility and Risks	Development plan/gradualness	2	2	2
Feasibility and Risks	Legal, procedures	2	2	3
Feasibility and Risks	Social support	1	1	3
Feasibility and Risks	Political support	2	1	2
Feasibility and Risks	Support other stakeholders	1	3	3

Source: CAREC Secretariat.

The main benefit of the MCA matrix is obviously the ability to show transparently, besides the results of standard evaluation models, different nonmonetary, nonquantifiable effects, including their scores/rankings, as well their feasibility aspects and risks. These feasibility aspects and risks do not directly link to the 3Ps, but form an important foundation to assess a project's readiness and viability.

Ranking of Projects

Based on the description above, a prioritization structure would look like the effect matrix presented in Table A5.2. This matrix can be very helpful in discussing and selecting priority projects from a wide range of options. Naturally, not all project options may have been evaluated in detail yet. Those will consequently have a lower score in 'readiness'. And any preliminary results of the CBA may be given a lower score compared to options that have been thoroughly evaluated. Options that lack key data (may be given score of zero or a negative score, depending on the scoring methodology applied.

Attributing the range of maximum scores for each indicator or effect enables a distinction in relative importance. For example, for CAREC railway corridors, aspects such as international competitiveness and intermodal connectivity will be relatively more important, compared to an evaluation of domestic passenger lines that serve domestic needs only. The actual methodology of the MCA may vary, as long as the application and ranking is done consistently.

Furthermore, it may be necessary to set a *minimum score* for a certain aspect, such as a threshold value of the EIRR. Similarly, one can add minimum scores for a group of effect, e.g. by disqualifying projects that score less than 10 in the feasibility and risk analysis.

Table A5.2: Example Effects Matrix and Project Ranking

				A	B	C	D	Range of rating	
	Project name or number			…	…	…	…		
		Sector		rail	rail	road	multimodal		
	Budget claim								
Results Financial and Economic CBA		Total investment value (fin.)	mln €	121	34	56	112		
		Investment value (econ.)	mln €	89	31	49	92		
		Score (financial)		0	10	5	0	0–5–10	
	Financial results								
		FIRR	%	–5.50%	0.20%	1%	–6%		CBA
		Score		0	5	5	0	0–5–10	
	Economic results								
		EIRR	%	8.10%	14%	5%	6%		
		VOT-savings	mln €	1.2	3.3	0.6	0.5		
		Accident-cost savings		0.5	0.3	0.6	0.1		
		Environmental cost savings		0.7	0.2	0.4	0.3		
		Score (based on EIRR)		10	20	0	10	0–10–20	
	Score subtotal CBA			10	35	10	10	**0–20–40**	**40%**
Profit	Accesibility infrastructure networks/multimodality			0	2	4	4	0–2–4	
	Improvement international competitiveness			1	2	1	1	0–1–2	Multi-Criteria Analysis
	Impact regional economy			0	3	3	6	0–3–6	
	Impact national economy			0	0	2	0	0–2–4	
People	Employment opportunities (long-term)								
		Region		1	1	0	0	0–1–2	
		Outside region		0	0	2	1	0–1–2	
	Strengthening social infrastructure			1	0	1	2	0–1–2	
	Improvement physical living environment			2	2	0	0	0–1–2	
Planet	Environmental benefits (other, nonquantified)			2	1	1	1	0–1–2	
	Climate effect			1	1	1	1	0–1–2	
	Landscape quality effects			2	0	0	0	0–1–2	
	Score subtotal unquantified effects 3Ps			10	12	15	16	**0–15–30**	**30%**

continued on next page

Table A5.2 continued

		A	B	C	D	Range of rating	
Feasibility and Risks	Overall readiness (ongoing, studies, preparation, etc.)	4	4	0	2	0–2–4	**Multi-Criteria Analysis**
	Technical risks	0	2	2	4	0–2–4	
	Legal framework (obstacles)	1	0	0	1	0–1–2	
	Market risk (dependency, fluctuation)	2	2	2	2	0–2–4	
	Exploitation opportunities (transfer)	1	0	0	0	0–1–2	
	Innovation	1	0	0	0	0–1–2	
	Political support	0	2	0	4	0–2–4	
	Social support	4	2	0	0	0–2–4	
	Project robustness	2	0	1	2	0–1–2	
	Project flexibility	2	1	1	0	0–1–2	
	Score subtotal feasibility and risk profile	17	13	6	15	*0–15–30*	30%
Total overall score		37	60	31	41	0–50–100	100%
	Priority ranking overall result	3	1	4	2		

CBA = cost–benefit analysis, EIRR = economic rate of return, FIRR = financial rate of return, VOT = value of time.
Source: CAREC Secretariat.

Important to note is that prioritization of CAREC rail infrastructure projects is not a one-time, static exercise, but requires regular updates based on progress made in project preparation. The evaluation and prioritization methodology can be improved and fine-tuned overtime.

Advantages of Effects Matrixes

In summary, the main advantages of applying an effect matrix as described in this section are:

(i) **Transparency:** a complete and distinct review of several projects can be shown in one page, facilitating discussion and decision-making.
(ii) It makes a clear **distinction** between **monetary** and **nonmonetary** criteria and between quantifiable and nonquantifiable criteria.
(iii) It can include an internalization (monetization) of **external effects** of transport.
(iv) The structure, indicating the relative importance of each effect, helps to **define the level of detail** the ranking should treated with; in other words, don't spend elaborate (costly) analyses on qualitative criteria that only defines a maximum of e.g. 1 or 2% of the total score.
(v) The requirements for underlying **feasibility studies** can already include and describe all the elements of the criteria list in advance.
(vi) The structure can be **easily adapted** to a specific context/type of projects or modality and altered on the basis of the experience gained overtime.

Internalization of the External Costs of Transport: Guidelines in Europe

As referred to earlier, one of the models to evaluate infrastructure projects is the economic cost–benefit analysis. In this analysis the economic cost[1] of an investment and related operation and maintenance costs[2] are being offset by the economic benefits. In case of a rail infrastructure project, these benefits consist of time savings of passengers and freight, and reduced car and truck operating cost (minus fares for alternative rail transport). However, since rail transport is more environmentally friendly compared to road transport, the positive external effects of rail transport can be 'internalized', meaning that they can be expressed in monetary terms and added to the benefits in the economic analysis.

The European Commission has initiated comprehensive research projects to enable this internalization. In 2008 the European Commission released its first handbook on estimation of external costs in the transport sector.[3] This handbook provided quantifications and monetary values by the European Union member country, and by mode of transport, such as those presented in Table A5.3.

In 2014, an update of the handbook continued to present state-of-the-art and best practice on external cost estimation, providing guidelines to include these in monetary terms in project evaluation. The total external cost savings of a rail infrastructure project can add 20%, 30% or even more to the monetary economic benefits. Projects that divert significant volumes of freight from road to rail transportation enjoy especially high benefits from external cost savings. Consequently, the inclusion of external cost savings in the economic evaluation is an effective instrument to promote sustainable rail transport.

---

[1] Economic costs are the financial cost after correction of price distortions, such as taxes, import and export duties and shadow wages.
[2] Depending on the organizational structure of the railway concerned, the producer's surplus can be separated into Operations and Infrastructure.
[3] CE Delft. 2008. *Handbook on Estimation of External Costs in the Transport Sector, Version 1.1.*

Table A5.3: Average External Costs in 2008 for EU-27 by Cost Category and Transport Mode (Excluding Congestion)

	Average Cost per Cost Category											
	Passenger Transport							Freight Transport				
	Road				Rail	Aviation	Total	Road			Rail	Waterborne	Total
Cost Category	Passenger cars €/(1,000 pkm)	Buses and coaches €/(1,000 pkm)	Motorcycle & mopeds €/(1,000 pkm)	Total road passenger transport €/(1,000 pkm)	Passenger transport €/(1,000 pkm)	Passenger transport (cont.) €/(1,000 pkm)	€/(1,000 pkm)	Light-duty vehicles €/(1,000 tkm)	Heavy-duty vehicles €/(1,000 tkm)	Total road freight transport €/(1,000 tkm)	Freight transport €/(1,000 tkm)	Freight transport €/(1,000 tkm)	€/(1,000 tkm)
Accidents	32.3	12.3	156.6	33.6	0.6	0.5	29.0	56.2	10.2	17.0	0.2	0.0	13.4
Air pollution	5.5	6.0	11.8	5.7	2.6	0.9	5.2	17.9	6.7	8.4	1.1	5.4	7.1
Climate change high scenario	17.3	9.1	11.1	16.3	1.5	46.9	17.6	44.5	9.8	14.9	0.9	3.6	12.1
Climate change low scenario	3.0	1.6	1.9	2.8	0.3	8.0	3.0	7.6	1.7	2.6	0.2	0.6	2.1
Noise	1.7	1.6	14.4	2.0	1.2	1.0	1.9	6.3	1.8	2.5	1.0	0.0	2.1
Up- and downstream high scenario	5.7	2.8	3.6	5.4	8.1	7.1	5.7	14.3	3.0	4.7	4.2	1.3	4.4
Up- and downstream low scenario	3.4	1.5	2.3	3.2	3.9	3.9	3.3	8.4	1.7	2.7	2.4	0.8	2.5
Nature and landscape	0.6	0.3	0.5	0.6	0.2	0.6	0.6	0.9	0.7	0.7	0.0	0.4	0.6
Biodiversity losses	0.2	0.4	0.1	0.2	0.0	0.1	0.2	0.6	0.5	0.5	0.0	0.5	0.4
Soil and water pollution	0.3	0.9	0.3	0.4	0.5	0.0	0.4	1.8	0.8	1.0	0.4	0.0	0.8
Urban effects	1.0	0.4	0.8	0.9	0.6	0.0	0.8	3.1	0.5	0.9	0.1	0.0	0.7
Total (high scenario)	64.7	33.8	199.2	65.1	15.3	57.1	61.3	145.6	34.0	50.5	7.9	11.2	41.7
Total (low scenario)	48.1	24.9	188.7	49.4	9.8	15.0	44.3	102.8	24.6	36.1	5.3	7.7	29.7

pkm = passenger-kilometer, tkm = ton-kilometer.
Source: CE Delft. 2011. *External Costs of Transport in Europe, Update Study for 2008*.

APPENDIX 6
CAREC Railway Data

Table A6.1: CAREC Railway Data, 2014

Country	Railway Length in Operation (km)	Gauge (mm)	Passengers Transported (million)	Passenger Transport Volume (million-passenger-km)	Freight Transported (million ton)	Freight Transport Volume (million-ton-km)	Number of Staff
Afghanistan	75	1,520	0.00	0	1.86	NA	NA
Azerbaijan	2,066	1,520	2.52	612	21.8	7,371	22,886
Georgia	1,994	1,520	2.73	550	16.67	4,947	12,700
Kazakhstan	14,205	1,520	20.50	18,300	275.30	216,500	76,240
Kyrgyz Republic	417	1,520	0.32	43	7.38	1,010	5,131
Mongolia	1,810	1,520	3.30	1197	21.12	12,473	13,364
Pakistan	7,791	1,676*	47.69	19,779	1.61	1,090	80,054
Tajikistan	680	1,520	0.46	20	6.81	448	5,770
Turkmenistan	2,313	1,520	6.00	1,685	25.00	11,547	18,701
Uzbekistan	4,593	1,520	17.30	3,673	65.00	22,918	58,239
(Subtotal)	35,944	–	100.82	45,859	442.55	278,304	–
PRC	111,821	1,435	2,357	1,160,475	3,813.34	2,753,019	2,003,306
PRC: Inner Mongolia Autonomous Region	10,226	1,435	47.89	20,173	651.65	236,761	–
PRC: Xinjiang Uygur Autonomous Region	5,462	1,435	23.29	22,019	74.10	84,360	–

CAREC = Central Asia Regional Economic Cooperation, PRC = People's Republic of China, km = kilometer, mm = millimeter, OSJD = Organization for Cooperation of Railways.

Note: * Includes 312 km of 1,000 mm gauge.

Source: CAREC Railway Working Group database. Where 2014 data not available, the most recent data available were used. For the number of staff, the data from OSJD were used except for Pakistan.

www.ingramcontent.com/pod-product-compliance
Lightning Source LLC
Chambersburg PA
CBHW060926170426
43192CB00025B/2909